SELLING YOUR BUSINESS
FOR ALL IT'S WORTH

If you want to know how...

Planning a Career Change
Rethink your way to a better working life

A Simple Guide to Pensions
*Discover how to solve the pension puzzle and provide
for a comfortable retirement*

Investing in Stocks & Shares
A step-by-step guide to making money on the stock market

Turning Your Business Around
*How to spot the warning signs and
keep your business healthy*

Send for a free copy of the latest catalogue to:

How To Books
3 Newtec Place, Magdalen Road,
Oxford OX4 1RE, United Kingdom
email: info@howtobooks.co.uk
http://www.howtobooks.co.uk

How to prepare your business for sale and get the best possible price

SELLING YOUR BUSINESS

FOR ALL IT'S WORTH

MARK BLAYNEY

howtobooks

Published by How To Books Ltd,
3 Newtec Place, Magdalen Road,
Oxford OX4 1RE. United Kingdom.
Tel: (01865) 793806. Fax: (01865) 248780.
email: info@howtobooks.co.uk
http://www.howtobooks.co.uk

The views expressed in this publication may not be those of LLoyds TSB plc.

British Library Cataloguing in Publication Data
A catalogue record for this book is available from the British Library

Edited by Diana Brueton
Cover design by Baseline Arts Ltd, Oxford
Produced for How To Books by Deer Park Productions
Typeset by PDQ Typesetting, Newcastle-under-Lyme, Staffs.
Printed and bound in Great Britain by Bell & Bain Ltd, Glasgow

NOTE: The material contained in this book is set out in good faith for general guidance and no liability
can be accepted for loss or expense incurred as a result of relying in particular circumstances on
statements made in the book. The laws and regulations are complex and liable to change, and readers
should check the current position with the relevant authorities before making personal arrangements.

ISBN: 1 85703 870 3

Contents

Introduction

WHY DO YOU NEED THIS BOOK?

Some people only ever sell their business once, typically when they are looking to retire. Others will find themselves selling their businesses a number of times during their careers as they move from one project to the next.

But both types of people have one thing in common, they both need to get the best deal possible out of the sale:

♦ if retiring, to secure the future
♦ if looking to move on, to fund the next venture.

This book is written to help you to ensure you get the best possible deal when you come to sell, for whatever reason.

WHAT DO YOU NEED TO DO TO GET THE BEST DEAL?

To get the best result from any sale requires preparation, having a structured approach to marketing what you have for sale, and negotiating the actual deal. Take for example selling a car. To get the best price you would generally need to:

♦ **Decide why you want to sell** – you need to have a convincing reason to tell prospective purchasers, such as trading up, otherwise they may think that it's a problem with the car that has led you to sell.

♦ **Pick the best time to sell** – so that you are selling at a time that suits you (rather than being forced into a sale when you are desperate for the money), and you are selling at the best time of year (eg you are likely to get more for your convertible in May than in November).

- **Do some market research** – to check how much your car is likely to be worth, what you want to get for it, how much you will ask (to give yourself some room for negotiation) and what seems to be the best way to advertise it.

- **Get the car and the supporting paperwork prepared** – so that the car is attractive, you have taken out anything you want to keep (or could sell for more separately), you have the HP paid off, you have the service record, MOTs, receipts and logbook to hand.

- **Start your marketing** – place your adverts and be available to take any calls.

- **Deal with enquiries** – meet prospective buyers, give out the right image about yourself as much as about the car and deal with their questions.

- **Let the buyer do their checks** – look under the bonnet and take a test drive.

- **Negotiate the price** – (how much) and the terms (cash or banker's draft, not personal cheque).

- **Complete the sale** – take cash and write out a pair of signed receipts (one for you to keep) describing the sale on an as seen basis to avoid any future claims; and send your part of the logbook in to the DVLC so that you don't start to receive demands for payment of the buyer's parking tickets or speeding fines!

The same general approach will apply to selling your business. Just bear in mind that when your buyer decides that they want an independent inspection of what they are buying, it's likely to be an ACA or ACCA (a Chartered or Certified Accountant) that turns up to look at the books (a '**due diligence**' report), not the AA to look at the engine.

SO WHAT IS SO DIFFICULT ABOUT SELLING A BUSINESS?

It's important to realise however that there are fundamental ways in which selling your business will differ from selling your car.

When you sell your car, you don't expect	But when you sell your business you may find
To worry about giving out information to prospective buyers about the car	You need to be careful about how much information you give out during the process, as for example, you don't want your main competitors picking up your key customer list for free
To worry about advertising that the car is for sale	You want to keep the fact that the business is for sale secret from suppliers, staff or customers until the deal is done
To be asked to lend the purchaser the money to buy the car	You have to allow the purchaser some credit to enable them to pay you in part over time out of the profits of what was your business ('vendor financing')
The final price to be uncertain until you have worked out exactly how much petrol is in the tank	The final price will have to include stock at valuation (**SAV**) at the date of sale
To be expected to have to give written confirmation that the car has not broken down in the last two years	You are asked to confirm some facts about your business in writing ('give warranties')
To be required to give your purchaser driving lessons	You have to agree to stay on for two weeks or two years to help train the purchaser in running your business or to smooth the introduction of the buyer to your customers
To promise the new owner that you won't buy a new car	You are asked to sign an undertaking not to set up business again in any way that will compete with the business you have just sold
The final price to be dependent on how well the car keeps running over the next two years	The price agreed includes clauses that adjust the total paid up ('escalators') or down ('clawbacks') based on future performance
To consider the tax implications of a sale	Tax planning may be vital to ensure you obtain the best net result from your sale
To need anyone else's permission to sell (assuming that you have paid off any hire purchase)	You may need agreement for the sale and transfer of assets or contracts from your landlord, franchiser, or even suppliers or customers with long-term contracts that include clauses covering change of business ownership

In addition, just as there are specific price guides, key criteria for valuing (make, model, age, condition and mileage), and specialist magazines for selling cars, there may be similar 'standard approaches' that are specific to your business, eg:

◆ Traditional routes to sale – such as specialist agents who deal with licensed premises, agricultural land agents or brokers who specialise in professional practices.

◆ Standard information required on which purchasers make decisions or on which businesses in your industry are valued – such as barrelage for pubs.

◆ Traditional sale terms – such as SAV ('stock at value') for pubs.

HOW WILL THESE ISSUES AFFECT YOUR BUSINESS?

The degree of complexity involved in the sale process and the issues arising from it will vary depending on the size and complexity of the business and the nature of the sale.

This book is therefore designed to address the whole range of situations just described, to help every seller achieve the best outcome and while not all the detail of each chapter will be relevant to every business sale, the general principles outlined will apply to all sales to some degree.

Most of the terms used in the book are defined in the text, and you will also find a glossary of relevant terms at the back of the book.

Type of business	Approach to selling	Will generally be selling to	And the sale may involve
A small husband and wife or lifestyle business such as a pub, small shop or guest house.	Might typically advertise for themselves in the small ads section of the relevant business press, or engage specialist estate agents.	Other individuals.	A quick hand-over. May require some form of vendor financing by the sellers, and a short period of 'on the job' training in running the business.
A small service business or professional practice such as a vets, dentists, accountants, estate agents or solicitors.	Might generally use a specialist firm of business brokers.	Other firms looking to expand (eg a 'consolidator'). Junior partners within the firm may have the option to buy out older partners who are looking to retire.	May require a period of consultancy of up to say two years to allow for an orderly hand-over of the trade and client base to the new owners. May involve some form of 'earn-out' where the price includes an element determined by future performance.
An established industrial business with a turnover of £2–5 million and ten to 20 staff.	Is likely to need to engage accountants to assist in preparing the business for sale, marketing the business and dealing with the purchaser's advisors.	Another business (such as a competitor in the industry) by way of a 'trade sale'. A team from within the business's existing management (a management **buy-out** or 'MBO') backed by venture capital (VC) firm.	The purchaser will employ accountants to undertake a detailed review of the business's financial position and trading performance and prospects (a 'due diligence report'). Payment in part by way of shares or options in an acquiring company ('paper') rather than cash.
A rapidly expanding high tech business with high growth plans.	Will need to engage a team of specialist corporate finance advisors to market a stake in the business to potential funders to raise money for the business's expansion.	A venture capital (VC) house looking for investment in the sector. A wealthy individual looking to invest in (and often to become actively involved as a director of) growing companies (a **'business angel'**).	Preparation of a detailed sales document (**'prospectus'**) requiring a range of projections and professionally prepared information that needs to comply with complex regulation. A complex range of capital instruments such as **preference** shares and/or options put in place as part of the new financing arrangements. Obtaining a **listing** that involves a number of external investors buying the company's shares such as an **Ofex** or **AIM** listing.

This book is therefore designed to address the whole range of situations just described to help every seller achieve the best outcome and while not all the detail of each chapter will be relevant to every business sale, the general principles outlined will apply to all sales to some degree.

Most of the terms used in the book are defined in the text, and you will also find a glossary of relevant terms at the back of the book.

DEDICATION

To my parents for all their support and Pat, as ever.

ACKNOWLEDGEMENT

I would like to thank Ian MacDonald of Ward Hadaway, George Moore of Regenesis Partners Ltd, and Adam Wardle of Horwath Corporate Finance for their assistance in reviewing the contents of this book, and Horwath Corporate Finance and Ward Hadaway for the use of sample documents.

Why Are You Selling?

WHY SELL?

There are many reasons why business owners choose to sell their business including a desire for retirement or to hand over succession to other family members, business partners or management.

Other reasons may include:

♦ To acquire money to fund growth, when the opportunities available to a business are greater than can be exploited by the business based on its own financial resources.

♦ To become associated with a larger firm, allowing access to their developed distribution channels or their particular manufacturing or marketing strengths.

♦ To allow concentration on a particular area of operations without having to worry about 'the whole shooting match'.

♦ To pursue other business interests.

♦ To reduce risk by 'banking' some or all of the cash made in building up the business, thereby eliminating some of the personal risks that will come from making future business decisions.

Whatever your reasons, you need to decide that you are serious about selling your business, as it is not a decision that should be taken lightly. After all, once your business is sold, it is sold. In addition, the process will take up an enormous amount of time and effort and will cause significant amounts of disruption to the business when customers, competitors, employees and suppliers find out that it is being sold.

Nevertheless, if you have successfully grown a business, sooner or later you are likely to consider selling it. In addition to disposing of all the worries and responsibilities, you will be looking to reap the financial rewards of all the hard work that you have put in over the years. However, the prospect of a sale for an entrepreneur (who has often founded the business) can create mixed emotions. On the one hand there is the prospect of realising the value of the business that has been built and obtaining both financial freedom and freedom from the demands, risks and worries of running a business. On the other hand, letting go of your baby which you have sweated and worried and slaved to build can generate a strong sense of loss, particularly if you feel responsible for the prospects of staff and managers left in the business.

Many owner-managers therefore find it harder than you might expect to decide whether or not they ought to be selling the business.

The principal reasons for selling divide into a number of personal and business requirements.

Banking the money

Often much of a business owner's personal wealth will be tied up in the company they have created. A sale of the business therefore offers the principal opportunity to convert this holding into cash which allows the business owner to diversify their investment across a range of different types of asset and investments, thereby minimising their exposure to the particular business's health or otherwise, and to enjoy the benefits of having created a successful business.

Reduction of risk

Often in the early days of a business, despite the legal status of limited liability, the owner finds that they have had to put up personal security in order to obtain bank funding, or even to give personal guarantees in order to obtain certain supplies, ranging from property leases all the way down to a photocopier. The effect of these personal guarantees is that the business owner is liable for the debts of the company in the event of the company's failure, and we often find that such personal guarantees, given in the early days of business, have never been fully removed. In addition, the responsibilities of directors grow ever more onerous with every piece of legislation and, for example in the event of **insolvency**, directors face the prospect of potentially being made personally liable for some of the company's trading losses. It makes sense therefore for owner-managers at some point to seek to reduce their exposure to such risks by selling the business to others who are willing to run it.

Health concerns or retirement

The above points are particularly relevant when the owner-manager decides it is time to retire or their health starts to fail. In fact, many businesses are sold not because of any financial considerations, but principally through some change in the owner's life; however many entrepreneurial business owner-managers seem to thrive on the activity and mental challenge of running their own business well into their 70s and later.

Boredom

Entrepreneurs and owner-managers are human, and they do get bored. Those who are highly entrepreneurial may find that once they have established a business they sooner or later become bored with running the same thing and wish to move on to new projects. Others become bored with living under the continual pressure, and decide they wish to pursue other interests, seek to retire, or occasionally, seek to hand on the administrative and managerial aspects to others in order to concentrate on the particular aspects that they love.

Money to grow

The faster your business is growing, the greater will be its demand for working capital to meet its expanding trading, together with investment capital to support it in exploiting new opportunities. For this type of company, achieving a sale of part of the owner's interest can be the route to acquiring the capital needed to take on the opportunities that arise, but this will naturally involve some form of loss of control of the business in return for the external capital introduced. In these circumstances an entrepreneur has to decide whether the opportunities offered by this extra money compensate for the restrictions on their independence.

Considering the implications

If you are thinking about selling, think through the implications for your personal life. How will you feel once you have sold up? What are you planning to do next? When deciding whether you wish to sell, you should consider the above motives. Which apply to you?

If you are considering retiring bear in mind that your business environment gives you a high degree of structure to your life. Moving to retirement will be a major change in lifestyle for which you need to prepare. Therefore seek out other business people who have sold up, and talk to them about both the process and the impact of having sold up on their lives, their relationships and what they have gone on to do.

GOLDEN RULE 1

Have a good reason to sell (that is logical to the buyer)
The buyer will want to know why you are selling. The more valid your reason
for selling, the more serious the buyer will be. If you do not appear to
have a valid reason for selling, the buyer will be suspicious and think you are
selling because there is something wrong with the business that they have not yet
spotted or you are not serious about selling. If they are suspicious about the
business they will not pay you as much for it.

KEEP YOUR BUSINESS OFF THE MARKET UNTIL YOU WANT TO SELL

Once you have decided whether you want to sell, the next question is
'When to sell?'

Some owners take the attitude that the business 'is always for sale'
for the right price. These businesses are not really interested in the
sale but if someone is prepared to make them a silly offer they would
consider it.

The problem with this approach is that a serious buyer with a serious
interest is committed to expending a high degree of cost in time and
cash in pursuing an offer through to a sale. Stop for a moment and
think how the 'we're always for sale if the price is right' approach
appears to a serious purchaser. They could spend a lot of time and
money pursuing the purchase of your business only to find, in the
last analysis, that you are not actually interested in selling it. This
may also mean that you miss out on what otherwise might be a good
offer.

Then bear in mind that often the most easily accessible buyers for your business (if not necessarily the best) will be somebody already in your trade. How small an industry do you work in? You may well find that word quickly gets round about those people who are 'always for sale but only for silly money', but who are 'not serious about going through with it'. If you get yourself tarred with this brush, you are unlikely to attract a serious buyer on the offchance that you are really going to go through with it this time.

Worse still, should you later decide (or are forced by circumstances) to attempt to really sell the business, how many purchasers in your industry, knowing this reputation, are going to take you seriously? In effect, therefore, you will already have spoilt part of the market.

Or worse again, if the market knows that the business has been for sale for a long period, it may come to be perceived as 'damaged goods' because many potential buyers will suspect that you haven't achieved a sale because there is something wrong with your business. If you get yourself into this situation, how successful are you going to be when it actually comes time to sell? And what price are you likely to attract?

GOLDEN RULE 2

Be serious about selling

Don't be for sale until you are for sale. Ensure that buyers know that they have a one-off opportunity to deal with a serious seller who is committed to go through with the process of selling and won't waste their time and money.

SO WHEN SHOULD YOU SELL?

You are likely to get the best price for your business at the point when its growth prospects appear highest. The growth prospects of your business will appear best when:

- your company's business is growing (has been growing strongly and has prospects of strong future growth)

- your industry is growing and

- the outside economy is growing.

Ideally, therefore, you want to be selling at a time when your performance is good and your prospects are better.

It is a fact of life that many entrepreneurs are attracted to high growth industry as an expanding market offers easier opportunities to create a new business. What you must bear in mind however is that every high growth industry eventually settles down to a much lower rate of growth which cannot support new entrants into the market and often cannot support all of the existing players. Therefore many sectors, from skateboard shops through to nursing homes, golf clubs, and mobile phone shops, will show periods of high growth with large numbers of players entering the field only to have a 'shakeout' as the rate of growth declines and the less successful players go to the wall.

In buying your business, purchasers will be putting a value on the prospects of the business.

When picking your moment to sell therefore, it pays to 'leave something in it for the next man'. Remember that selling a business is a process that will take some time. Many entrepreneurs are tempted to hang on into a growth industry, attempting to squeeze every drop of growth out of the business and aiming to sell right at the top of the curve (just before B in Figure 1). The danger with this approach is that you just might be very lucky and sell out at exactly the right time. However, bear in mind that the sales process will take several months to complete, from start to finish. The chances are that you will not be successful and will miss selling right at the peak.

The point to note here is that the value of the business at point A is likely to be much greater, or as great as the value of the business at point B because the business at point A is being valued on the basis of continuing growth as perceived in the marketplace; whereas the value of the business at point B is being valued on the basis of a flat market. Selling at point A may therefore get you a better price than selling at point B, as even though point B is higher, a buyer may 'overpay' at point A.

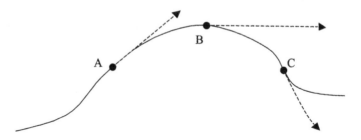

Figure 1. Buyers buy on trends.

Moreover, the value of the business at point C will be based on a declining market and although objectively the business is at the same level as at point A, a buyer will tend to underpay, based on the current declining trend.

You should review your business every six months or so and consider whether now is a good time to sell. In fact, asking yourself the question: 'Would people want to buy my company?' is a good test of whether you are generating value or not. Because if the answer is 'no', what does this tell you about your business?

Keep an eye, therefore, on the value of your business and the rate of growth of it, its industry and economy in general.

GOLDEN RULE 3

Choose your moment to sell, do not have it forced upon you
Be proactive about deciding when you want to sell your business. Never allow yourself to become a forced seller of your business as a result of economic or other reasons as you will achieve a worse price because first, you will not be selling at the most opportune moment to maximise value, and second, anxiety will force you to accept worse offers than you would otherwise consider.

WHAT IF YOU NEED TO SELL BUT YOUR BUSINESS IS IN DIFFICULTY?

If your business is in difficulty, should you attempt to sell it you must accept that you are unlikely to get as much for it as you would if it was in good health. As you are a distressed seller or selling a distressed business, the value you are likely to achieve for your business will be low.

Therefore, if your business is in difficulties, in order to improve the price you are likely to achieve, it may well be advisable to attempt to turn it around first so as to be able to market a business with a better current trading performance and future prospects.

If your business has become quite severely distressed, and in practice would fail one of the tests for insolvency set out in the Insolvency

Act 1986, in that it is unable to pay its debts as they fall due or that its liabilities exceed its assets, then there are further problems in attempting to achieve a sale. These are that, in the event of a liquidation, the insolvency practitioner who has been appointed will have a duty to look at transactions during the period leading up to the insolvency, particularly those undertaken when the company was technically insolvent, to see whether any of these should be reversed. In particular, they will be looking for transactions at undervalue where they are able to argue that an asset has been sold off cheaply (eg you have sold the Rolls Royce to Joe, your brother, for £5 the day before the liquidation), or preferences, where they are able to argue that you have acted to put one creditor in a better position than others (eg you have paid Joe, or have transferred assets to him in settlement of his account prior to the liquidation, when you have not paid other creditors).

Thus any sale or transfer of a business's assets in the period leading up to a liquidation may be subject to a challenge in the courts by a liquidator. They may also feature in the liquidator's report on the directors' conduct prepared for the DTI and upon which the DTI decide whether or not to take directors disqualification proceedings.

For further information about insolvency and business turnaround issues, try www.turnaroundhelp.co.uk or *Turning Your Business Around* (How To Books, ISBN 1-85703-767-7).

In addition, by taking as many of the steps suggested in this book as possible, even if over a reduced timescale, you will at least present your business for sale in its best possible light (known amongst the turnaround profession as 'polishing the pig').

GOLDEN RULES SUMMARY

1. Have a good reason to sell (that is logical to the buyer).

2. Be serious about selling.

3. Choose your moment to sell, do not have it forced upon you.

What is Involved in the Sales Process?

HOW LONG WILL IT TAKE TO SELL YOUR BUSINESS?

First and foremost, be prepared for the long haul, as the entire process of selling your business from start to absolute finish could take as long as nine years.

If this seems surprising then I'll say at once that this assumes a structured **grooming** and sales process of two or three years with a year in which to actually sell your business; whilst the rest of the prospective nine years relates to dealing with the aftermath.

To illustrate what I mean and to give a flavour of some of the issues covered in the rest of the book, set out below is a summary of the sales process that a normal mid-sized trading business might go through in order to obtain the best realisation.

Two to three years prior to sale

As a business owner you will need to seek recommendations as to good potential advisors, meet with them and discuss your plans with them.

Having done so, on the basis of the advice received from the advisors, you should start to **groom** the business for sale. This means ensuring that its trading performance is managed to demonstrate strong, reliable profits and growth. This may involve either restricting your drawings by way of salary, and abandoning other mechanisms used to reduce profits and hence tax paid, which will result in the business paying higher taxes than it used to; or at least keeping detailed records of all such issues with which to subsequently adjust the published profit and loss and to support these adjustments during the due diligence process.

This is a good moment to consider whether you are actually a serious seller as there is little point committing to paying higher taxes than you need to if you are subsequently not going to sell.

One year prior to sale

With the business trading and demonstrating good strong profits, it is time to tidy up the business's paperwork and reduce the risks, get all its contracts in order, negotiate any leases that are required for the ongoing trading of the business, tie in key employees and also to tidy up the physical plant, machinery, and property of the company so it appears well ordered and attractive to prospective purchasers when they come to look round.

Ensure that you have all your books and records up to date, with copies of management accounts to demonstrate your strong profits and tight controls. It may also make sense to undertake a mock due diligence exercise (effectively to undertake the sort of audit of your business that a purchaser will undertake during the sale process), so as to identify any potential legal or financial problems that the purchaser's advisors may find, so that these can be resolved prior to entering into actual sales negotiations.

Start of the sales process

Meet with your advisors to finalise their instructions and work with them to prepare the necessary information. The advisors will generate a list of potential purchasers from your knowledge of the industry and by searching commercially available databases. This list will need to be discussed with you and the strategy on approaching prospective purchasers agreed. At the same time, the advisors will put together a **sales pack** which you will need to approve and, you will need to have discussed with them the valuation of the business and agree both your target price and a price below which you are not prepared to go.

Months two to three of the sales process

Your advisors will be out approaching the prospective purchasers, seeking to find whether they are actually interested in buying your business or not. On a regular basis, the advisors should be meeting with you to update you on progress, the responses received and any other prospective purchasers who may be added to the target list. At the same time, for those prospective purchasers who have expressed an interest, confidentiality agreements will be being sent out for signature and return, to allow sales packs to be despatched and discreet site visits arranged for those who are interested.

Months four to six of the sales process

By this stage your advisors should be pressing interested parties to make their initial offers, which should then be discussed with you, so that between you and your advisors, you prioritise those interested parties who are serious and most likely to do an acceptable deal, so that your advisors can concentrated on these.

Further site visits are likely to take place and interested parties will be looking for more information to be provided which may require you to set up a **data room** (an office where information will be available to prospective purchasers to look through), either somewhere on your site, or more often off-site with your advisors.

Meanwhile your advisors will be continuing to negotiate widely with a range of potential interested parties and construct their strategy for conducting the sale eg should they conduct an auction, grant exclusivity or move to a 'best and final bids' in order to ensure they obtain the best offer.

However, by the close of this period you need to be assessing the offers available and looking to negotiate with one, or possibly two, interested parties in order to achieve an agreement on price, and so produce a formal offer known as **heads of terms** or **heads of agreement**.

Months seven to nine of the sales process

Protected by an **exclusivity clause** in the heads of agreement, in parallel the buyer undertakes their detailed **due diligence review** of the business whilst the terms of the final sales contract are negotiated.

Any issues arising out of the due diligence will be being fed into the contract negotiations until a final contract can be drawn up by the solicitors which is why it is best to have cleared up the many issues as can be identified well in advance of this stage.

The buyer then completes the final closing due diligence, the contract is signed and on completion day all the actions take place which are needed to conclude the deal, such as transfer of the funds, and valuation of the stock. It is worth noting that in the sale of a distressed business, this timetable may need to be considerably shortened.

One to two years post sale

The sales contract is likely to include provisions that for a period of say, one or two years after the sale, the purchaser will have the right to claim back monies from the seller based on the warranties and representations given in the event that they find problems with the purchased business for which they may file claims under the terms of the contract.

In connection with this, part of the purchase price may be held on trust by a solicitor in an **escrow** account that can only be released at the end of the potential claim period. Conversely, the seller may need to stay on with the business, working for the buyer under a consultancy contract in order to ensure a smooth handover, and may even be entitled to receive further monies for a period of years following the sale under a form of escalator or earn-out clause if the business performs well.

Up to five years post sale

In order to protect the purchaser from the seller immediately going into competition with the new owners using the seller's old network of contacts, most sales contracts will include clauses that prevent the seller from setting up in similar businesses in the locality for a significant period, often up to five years although the longer this period, the more difficult such claims are to enforce.

Therefore, as you can see, whilst a normal corporate sales process is itself a fairly long drawn-out affair, typically lasting up to say nine months, to get the best result requires a significant period of prior preparation over something like two or three years, whilst the full financial and contractual implications of the sale may well take two to five years to completely work through. Thus, from having decided that you might like to sell your business to having completed the entire affair, may in some cases take almost a decade.

GOLDEN RULE 4

Start early

You are only going to sell this business once, so it does pay to do it right first time. This sale is like any other sales process, you have to know your product, prepare it so it is attractive for prospective customers, get to know the needs and wants of your prospective purchasers, and sell them the product, pursuing it all the way through to doing to deal.

ITEMS TO CONSIDER WHEN PLANNING TO SELL YOUR BUSINESS

Since the sale of the business is also the biggest sale the business will ever do, you have to commit time and effort to preparing the business for sale in order to find the right buyer and maximise the value you are going to get out of it. And since it will require an effort, it is worthwhile thinking in a structured way about what your goals are for selling the business, as set out below.

◆ What do you personally want out of the sale and what are your main reasons for wanting to sell the company?

◆ What do you want out of the sale for you, your company, your employees, or your management team? Would it matter to you, for example, if following a sale the purchaser shut your business down? Or relocated it? Or are you determined that your company should continue on after you?

◆ Do you have children in the business? Do you want to ensure they have a role going forwards?

◆ Are you looking to stay with the business after the sale, either permanently, or for a period, or are you looking for a clean break and an exit?

◆ Do you want to retain any particular assets, such as the land and buildings, or any particular contracts?

◆ If you are selling in order to help your business develop, what characteristics are you looking for in the purchaser? And what are the reactions of your customers likely to be?

◆ What sort of terms of a deal would be best suited to you and your financial situation from a tax and pension planning point of view?

The sales process is important. Like anything else, sales are unlikely to come to you. You will have to go out and sell your business in the same way as you sell anything else. And just as when your company is selling products it is selling them in competition with other companies, when you come to sell your company you will find you are in competition with other people who are looking to sell their businesses to purchasers who have the money. Be prepared so as to give yourself the best chance of success.

WHAT ABOUT A FLOAT?

A flotation of a business (sometimes known by its US term of an **IPO**, or initial public offering), really represents simply a specialist type of sale, where rather than selling the whole business to one particular party, shares in the business are offered for sale into a marketplace where they can be freely traded.

Many businesses that I speak to talk about 'working towards a flotation' and they may see this and the liquidity it will generate as the end objective.

This is a mistake, as a few moments reflection from the point of view of prospective investors will clearly show. If the management team who have built the business and grown it to the stage where it can be floated simply want to exit at this stage, why should I, as an investor, put money into buying something where the factor which has been key to its growth so far is disappearing to the south of France with a fat wad of money in their back pocket?

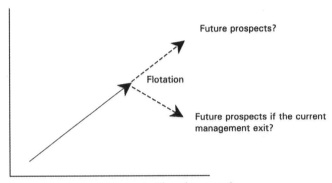

Figure 2. Flotation as exit.

No, a flotation must be seen as a tool for attracting more money to achieve the business's long-term goals. To be successful, it must clearly be an integral long-term part of the planned future development of the business, and can be presented as a way to raise funds for future investment in the business in order to secure future opportunities.

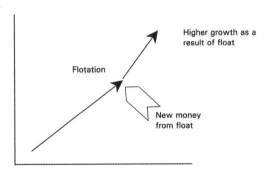

Figure 3. Successful flotation.

Preparation of a business for a flotation is probably worth a book in itself, but suffice it to say that many of the aspects of grooming a business for sale covered in this book will equally apply to a business looking to float. In addition, a management team that is looking to achieve a successful float must really run their business in terms of:

- management information
- investor relations
- strong financial management of the business with regard to return
- strategic planning, and
- corporate governance
- hiring of non-executives on the board as 'independent outsiders'.

in the way that a fully listed PLC would, for a good period (say at least three years) prior to obtaining a full listing.

Thus investors and analysts who deal with existing listed companies and are therefore used to seeing compliance with governance codes such as Cadbury, the provision of financially appropriate information to investors and a strong integrated strategy in the businesses in which they are investing, will be reassured to see these in place in your business as you bring it to market.

GOLDEN RULES SUMMARY

4. Start early.

What is Your Business Worth?

VALUATIONS ARE VALUELESS

The fundamental reason for buying and the one which drives most consideration of valuation, is to make money from the business.

Business valuation is a mix of art and science and, how much a buyer will be prepared to pay can depend not only on the nature and finances of your business, but also on the nature and finances of theirs.

In addition the strategic reasons that buyers may have for wanting to acquire your business can include:

- to rapidly enter a new market
- to rapidly increase market share in an existing market
- to take out a competitor
- to turn around a loss-making business
- to acquire new technology or other significant asset.

In some cases therefore, as a result of the buyer's reason for wanting to buy, the amount of money they are prepared to pay for a business bears absolutely no relation to any 'normal' valuation of the business. Three examples of real sales illustrate this point.

Case study 1 – The strategically important niche

The business manufactured a basic commodity product, the characteristics of which tended to mean that in any particular geographical area there would only be one supplier as a result of both the scale of operation required and the costs of moving finished goods over long distances.

The industry had therefore grown up based on a network of independent producers, each dominant in their own local territory but now consolidating. Essentially there were now two big players who were expanding by purchasing the local operators. One consolidator was expanding from south to north, the other was moving from west to east.

This particular business was one of the last independent operators and was located in the north east. As a basic commodity business with little perceived scope for adding on extra services or new uses, there was no perceived interest from players outside the industry. For the two expanding companies, however, the business was potentially a key strategic acquisition in terms of establishing who was going to be the dominant regional supplier.

The owners of the business had had a valuation done based on some of the techniques concerning current and future profitability discussed in this and the following chapter.

In practice, we adopted a strategy that was potentially dangerous in that we arranged for representatives of both consolidators to visit the factory on the same day. In doing so, each saw that the other was potentially interested in purchasing the business.

The risk in this strategy was twofold in that either they might get together and combine to offer a joint bid, with a view to cooperating in running the business as a joint venture or agreeing to split it up at some later date, having used this technique to drive down the price that the seller could obtain. Alternatively they might each resent being forced into competition and decide to sit out the bid. In practice what happened was that one of the consolidators decided to do exactly that and refused to enter a bid. This left us exposed so that if one consolidator knew the other was no longer in the running, they could put in a low bid knowing they had no competition.

However, it was not in the other consolidator's interests to allow its rival to snap up the business cheaply, so they kept quiet about the fact that they had dropped out of the bidding. In the event, the west-east consolidator ended up making an offer for the business including a number of assets they did not really want, at 50% greater than the expected valuation the company had obtained in the first place. They did so in order to ensure that it did not fall into the hands of their rivals because it was such a key strategic fit.

In practice, the acquisition proved not to be a success partly because they had overpaid; partly because in planning what they were going to do after the acquisition they had failed to adequately plan for the investment required to upgrade the company's facilities; but most importantly they had failed to undertake proper commercial due diligence in respect of the people issues. Following the acquisition they had put in place a management team that had rapidly come into conflict both with the new owner's main board and the staff within the company acquired due to mismatch of cultures. The result is that the business performed extremely poorly following the acquisition.

Case study 2 – The hidden asset
The business manufactured and sold a type of drinks dispenser

together with the consumables supplied to go into it. It was a relatively small operation that was essentially a one-man band who ran it as a 'lifestyle' business. The business was sold in a relatively straightforward way and the seller was pleased to obtain a significant premium over the value he was expecting.

As a matter of interest, the advisors followed up the sale some six months later, asking the purchasers how they were getting on and what sales they were obtaining of the product. The response from the purchasers was somewhat surprising, being to the effect: 'Actually we don't really know what we are getting in terms of sales of the product, but really we aren't that bothered.' The reason for this indifference was fairly simple, the purchasers had not purchased the business to obtain the existing trade (i.e. its sales of its drinks dispenser and the consumables). Whilst the purchaser was happy to have those sales, the real value of the deal to the purchaser was the distribution network and the opportunity it gave to get into the companies who were buying the company's drinks product. In fact, the purchaser was using this distribution network as an additional sales channel for its own core products and through this distribution network was now selling over ten times the value of its own products (non drinks) in comparison with the sales the **target** company's drinks dispensing consumables had ever achieved.

The value of the business to the purchaser was therefore nothing to do with the underlying trading ability of the company and its own products, but rather to do with its potential as a sales channel.

Case study 3 – Pride and prejudice
And you should never underestimate the personal element in respect of any purchase. *Takeovers* (Fallon, Ivan, and Srodes; James,

London, Hamish Hamilton 1987) covers many of the big business bidding battles of the 1980s and is filled with examples where winning a contest to buy a business became a matter of ego and pride for aggressive chief executives, and therefore where the commercial logic and questions of return on the investment seem to have gone out of the window.

Following the collapse of the Socialist bloc, I was involved in selling 'bust' businesses in a previously Socialist country. One of the cases involved a toilet paper manufacturer, which was in such a poor state that the machinery could no longer reliably put the perforations into the rolls.

Nevertheless, we marketed the business and quickly obtained a very strong offer to purchase it which gave us a significant premium over any reasonable 'normal' valuation of the business. A number of months following the sale I contacted the new local manager to enquire how the business was progressing and whether the buyer was happy with his purchase.

The reply was that the new owner would be happy with the purchase even if it was making no toilet rolls. In discussion, the background then came out. Before liberalisation, under the country's planned economy, every factory or operation had had to be licensed by the authorities to operate. The purchaser had applied for a licence to set up a toilet paper manufacturing company and the authorities had agreed that the country needed one such factory. He had started to set up in business when, to his surprise, the licence to operate such a factory was awarded to someone else, without any expertise in producing paper, but with good political connections. The purchaser had then travelled abroad and set up (successfully) in business elsewhere.

The news that this toilet paper business, which he had always regarded as having been stolen from him, had now collapsed, was bust, and was available to be purchased at a price that was (for him) a bargain, represented a chance to get his revenge upon both the licensing authorities and the person he believed had stolen the business from him in the first place.

Valuing issues

From the above three cases, you can clearly see that in addition to what might be considered the normal commercial justification for buying a business in respect of the business's 'own' business and its prospects for making money, there may be strategic issues for a purchaser in terms of snapping up a key territory or getting access to channels down which it can pass its own merchandise; or very personal matters, which can lead a purchaser to pay significantly more than might otherwise be expected for a business as it stands.

Valuing a private business is a particularly difficult exercise. Whilst a publicly listed company will be valued every day by the stock markets of the world, no actively traded market exists for your particular business until the day you decide to put it up for sale.

There are, however, a variety of financial bases for valuing businesses that will give a range of possible valuations depending on the assumptions used. The bases of these approaches to valuation are detailed in Chapter 4.

So, if financial based valuations give a range of values which may in the end be completely irrelevant to the value the purchaser places on the business and is therefore prepared to pay, why have a valuation at all?

GOLDEN RULE 5

Remember a valuation is just a valuation, your business is really worth (only) what someone is prepared to pay for it

At best a valuation is an opinion (i.e. a best guess) as to what someone will pay for your business. The only true valuation with any real meaning is the deal that is actually eventually done when someone puts their hand in their pocket to pay. This may sometimes reflect issues that are completely outside a normal valuation basis.

THE VALUE OF VALUATIONS

Nevertheless, it is useful to have a valuation exercise done as part of the process at the outset. The exercise in quantifying the potential value of the business to others can help you in:

- Identifying assets which you would rather keep than sell (eg the land and buildings) and might therefore be best excluded from the sale.

- Identifying financial risks existing in the current business (eg your personal guarantee of the bank overdraft) which will need to be dealt with by way of the sale.

- Identifying how best to groom the business for sale so as to get the best price.

◆ Understanding the range of possible valuations that will be placed on the business by different purchasers and the basis on which they and their advisors will arrive at these (which obviously also helps you on how to groom the business for sale to achieve the best price).

◆ Ensuring you have a realistic expectation of the price achievable for your business.

◆ Helping you quantify the price below which you are not prepared to go (your 'drop-dead' price) as it makes more sense to continue in business.

GOLDEN RULE 6

Decide on your drop-dead price in advance

In addition to your target price for the business, you also need in mind a drop-dead price which is the amount below which you will not sell. Obviously this is a figure which you never, repeat *never*, disclose to the prospective purchaser.

The buyer's advisors will, in any event, be undertaking a valuation exercise to assist the purchaser in deciding whether or not to make the investment. They will be using the same valuation methods as your advisors will be using to advise you how much it might sell for. Therefore, by undertaking the exercise you have the basis for discussion between the professional advisors.

Valuations will generally be done on a 'cash now' basis, which may not necessarily reflect the actual cash value of the eventual deal, as the payment terms of the actual deal done may differ significantly from an all cash offer.

GOLDEN RULE 7

Set a reasonable target price

Whatever valuation method you use, you should set a reasonable target price for your business. Setting a ridiculously high price can be a major mistake as:

◆ it may well scare away many potential buyers

◆ it tells people you are not very serious about selling your business

◆ it means your business may remain for sale for quite some time, which may lead potential buyers to think there is something wrong with your business which is preventing it from being sold; and

◆ it may well sour your post-deal relationship with the purchaser, which is a particular concern if you are expecting to have some involvement with the business after the sale.

THE DANGER OF OVER-RELIANCE ON VALUATIONS

As a general word of warning, before getting into price negotiations with a prospective purchaser you should have engaged professional assistance experienced in such negotiations.

Example

A **trade purchaser** was looking to buy some businesses in a particular sector and approached company A to see whether it might be for sale.

Company A was interested in selling.

The owner of company A spoke to his accountant, who advised him that he understood the business would normally be worth twice its annual profits. So company A started the conversation with the prospective purchaser by saying: 'My accountant thinks my business is potentially worth £X.'

The result was that £X became the starting point from which the purchaser was looking to negotiate the price downwards. The inevitable result was that the business could only be sold for something less than £X.

Having spoken to the accountant and obtained the valuation, what he should have done was to decide to keep this figure in mind as its bottom line drop-dead figure and engaged a corporate finance advisor. The corporate finance advisor would then make contact with the enquiring company and say: 'My clients are interested in discussing the sale of their business to you, and would like you to make an offer for it.'

The result of this approach would be that in order to proceed, the acquiring company has to give an indication of either the sum of money it is thinking about paying, or the basis on which that sum will be calculated. Therefore, if the purchasing company has specific reasons for wanting to acquire the business which would lead it to pay more than the 'normal' multiple mentioned by the accountant (as in the cases already discussed), their offer price might be significantly in excess of the accountant's estimated valuation. The company can then start negotiations without having given away either its bottom line or its target price.

GOLDEN RULE 8

First one to mention price, loses

As with all negotiations, it is usually best to wait for the other party to mention price first so as to avoid under or overpricing and to get some indication of their possible range of values.

Having both a target price and a drop-dead price in mind during negotiations will make these negotiations more effective. You will be able to kill negotiations that are not going to deliver your drop-dead price. Once you have achieved your target price this gives you the basis on which to consider the risks of continuing to negotiate in the hopes of getting a deal that significantly exceeds it, versus the benefits to be gained by accepting and moving to close a deal that achieves, or slightly exceeds, your target price.

Don't blow a good deal by being greedy.

BASIS OF VALUATION

There are six broad bases of valuation, many of which are however interlinked. These are:

Asset valuation	Total of the value of all the individual assets, tangible and intangible, in the business.
Market valuation	A comparison against the prices achieved for other businesses that have sold recently.
Discounted cashflow	Takes estimates of cash to be generated by the business in future years and uses accounting techniques to discount these back to a present value (or an implied internal rate of return that investing in the purchase of your business will generate for the acquirer).
Return on investment	Essentially creates ratios of either the return (the earnings that the purchaser will achieve) divided by the price they pay for your business, or the price/earnings ratio (which is the price they pay for your business divided by the current earnings stream) which shows how long it will take to repay the investment.
Sector specific	Particular sectors will have their own rules of thumb about how to value a business based on the characteristics of the business (eg the number of beds in the hotel, pub barrelage, value of mineral reserves, multiples of fee income).
Basic multiple	As a rule of thumb businesses with certain characteristics will be valued at a certain multiple of earnings.

These valuation terms are explained in more detail in Chapter 4.

WHAT'S FOR SALE?

In order to sensibly look at the valuation, however, you need to first consider the fundamental question: 'What is it you are looking to sell?' There are three key considerations that affect this.

What type of sale will it be?

There are two principal methods for selling an incorporated business (ie a limited liability company). You can either sell the company by selling the shares in it, or the company can sell the business and assets the company owns.

While this raises a number of issues, for the purpose of considering valuation at this stage it is enough to note that you as an owner may well prefer to sell your shares (ie the company) since this will generally lead to a single tax hit in respect of Capital Gains Tax on the value of the shares (see Chapter 13).

However, a purchaser may wish to buy the business and assets from the company, rather than the company itself, so as to enable them to acquire the individual assets at 'fair value' for incorporation on their balance sheet. This approach also helps the purchaser in restricting the potential for taking on unknown or **contingent liabilities** as part of the deal.

The difficulty for you in a sale of the business and assets is that obviously the company may be taxed on the proceeds of its sale of the business and assets, and then you may face tax again on attempting to get the proceeds of the sale out of the company and into the hands of the shareholders. You may therefore seek to get the purchaser to pay a higher value for the right to buy the business and assets rather than the shares.

What assets are included?

The second principal consideration affecting value is what in particular is for sale? For example, it is not uncommon, particularly in say retirement sales of family owned businesses, for the property from which the business is operated to be retained by the existing business owner and an arrangement made to rent the property to the owner of the new business, so as to provide an income stream for the business owner in retirement. Obviously the value of the business that has its own freehold property will be different from the value of a business that has to rent its property from the previous owner as a landlord.

What liabilities are the new owners going to acquire?

As the owner-manager of a business you may well have had to guarantee certain of the company's borrowings, such as an overdraft, or perhaps leases. When you sell the business on to another party, you will want to ensure that your liability is extinguished. Therefore, the impact of a commitment to repay the overdraft, or settle the outstanding leases, is part of the deal, and will need to be factored into the valuation, together with the impact of meeting over time the company's normal business obligations such as payment of existing trade creditors.

DO YOU HAVE A SALEABLE BUSINESS?

Many people, such as a consultant I worked with who was earning £350,000 in a good year, build up successful businesses that provide them with a good income but which are, however, inherently unsaleable.

If you have a business that is completely based upon your personal network of contacts or upon your personal skills, whilst this may be a successful business and provide you with a good living, it is essentially a lifestyle rather than a saleable business. This is because you are, in essence, the business. Crucially, the business has no life outside of you and your skills and contacts. Therefore there is nothing for anyone to buy, as on your retirement those people who come to you because of your contact with them will have no reason to come to the person who has bought your business.

Similarly, if people come to your business because of your specialised knowledge, why should they come to the business once you are no longer there?

Nevertheless such businesses will often have quite a powerful niche presence or name in their particular industry and so the owners expect to be able to sell them at a good value.

If you have such a business and you wish to be able to sell it, you need to take steps to 'institutionalise' your knowledge or contacts into the business so that the business has some life outside of you.

So, if the business is based around a personal contact network, you need to take steps to formalise this network into some form of database, setting out which customers and contacts provide which sort of lead or service. You need to engage sales staff in order to use this contact database and generate more income independent of your personal working of this network. From this you can look to develop the business's brand name such that people who aren't directly known to you or who come across your business through third parties or through reputation will start to use the business.

Similarly, if the business is built around your own specialist knowledge, again in order to have something which is worthwhile to sell, you will have to start to institutionalise this into a database of information, operating systems, processes, or some other mechanisms whereby the value of what you know can be transferred to others.

In practice the people for whom this will have most obvious value will be the people you bring in to your business, perhaps at first as employees or junior partners who you may then allow to buy you out over time.

Of course there are risks in moving from a one-man band to a business with a structure and a greater number of employees. Not least, where you are attempting to transfer the knowledge or contacts which form the basis of your business into a form that can be transferred to others they are therefore potentially at risk of being used by others without due benefit to yourself. As a result, part of the process of protecting what you are doing will be to ensure that staff being brought in sign proper terms and conditions that allow you to prevent them using any knowledge passing across them without having paid for it.

GOLDEN RULES SUMMARY

5. Remember a valuation is just a valuation, your business is really worth (only) what someone is prepared to pay for it.
6. Decide on your drop-dead price in advance.
7. Set a reasonable target price.
8. First one to mention price, loses.

4

Valuation Techniques

DO YOU NEED TO KNOW ABOUT VALUATIONS?

Most business valuations will need to be undertaken by the relevant professionals and you will therefore not need to be a master of all the technicalities of how to come up with valuations. For those who would prefer to avoid the detail, a summary of the principle methods is set out at the end of the chapter.

However, it is probably useful to have an understanding of how each valuation is arrived at, how they are used and their relative strengths and limitations so as to be able to deal properly with your professional advisors.

RESTATEMENT OF EARNINGS

As most valuations are based on estimated future earnings, one thing to appreciate (as covered in Chapter 5 on grooming for sale), is that the professional advisors will almost always make significant adjustments to either your past or projected future earning statements in coming to a valuation or preparing documents to show to prospective purchasers. This is a normal part of the process and will be accepted by experienced purchasers.

Business owners, particularly in small or family owned companies, are not normally motivated to manage their company's results to demonstrate the highest possible levels of earnings. Instead, they are generally motivated to manage their business and earnings in such a way as to minimise the tax payable, and it is fair to say that the degree to which business owners will 'manage' the figures to reduce the amount of tax they have to pay ranges from the completely legitimate, to the marginal, and right through to the completely illegitimate.

An important part of the grooming process is often therefore to manage earnings for a period to demonstrate the true profitability of the business. If this means paying higher levels of tax than you have been used to, you should console yourself with the thought that since the sale price you will achieve will probably be based on a multiple of earnings, you should get this extra tax paid back many times over.

The normal sorts of 'legitimate' profit management that your advisors will be looking to adjust in order to show as high a level as possible of underlying sustainable profit for valuation purposes and persuade the purchaser that they should pay a high valuation for the business, include:

◆ salary for yourself as business owner set at a high level so as to soak up all available profits and avoid double taxation, or for family members working in the business (eg your spouse)

◆ high levels of fringe benefit for family members, such as expensive cars

◆ above market rents charged to the company for use of property owned by you or your family personally.

In addition to the above, business owners may well also have been undertaking practices such as:

- paying salaries to family members who have absolutely nothing to do with working in the business

- charging personal expenditure such as pleasure trips to the business

- putting assets bought for personal use (such as a home computer) through the company, etc.

To obtain a realistic picture of the sustainable level of earnings of the business, all such elements will have to be stripped out and replaced where appropriate, with reasonable open market estimates of, for example, a director's salary, as someone has to run the business, and market rent for the building.

ASSET VALUATION

Since the purchaser is acquiring the assets of the business, the value of the assets often seems a logical place to start when valuing a business.

Indeed, for businesses that are loss-making or that have failed, it is normally the fundamental basis on which valuations are based, because if the company is loss-making, it has no stream of profits to multiply or project in order to generate any of the other forms of valuation.

There are essentially three bases of valuation of assets. These are **book value, going concern** and **forced sale value**.

Book value

Book value represents the total value of all the assets (net of the relevant liabilities) as stated in the company's accounts. It is also referred to as net asset value or net worth.

However, you should never confuse these accounting 'values' with real values. Accounts are based on a convention of historical cost, which means that an asset is booked into your accounts at the time you bought it. You will then generally have applied a depreciation policy that writes off the cost of the asset over the specific period of its useful life. The net book value of that asset in your accounts is therefore its original cost less the depreciation you have charged against it over the years since you bought it. The resulting 'book value' may be accurate from an accounting point of view, but you cannot rely on it bearing any resemblance to the **open market value** of the asset involved.

For example, computers are generally depreciated over three years, however the second hand value of computer equipment the day after you have opened the box may be a very small percentage of the cost of the new equipment the day before. Conversely, a property you bought many years ago, and which you have been depreciating slowly over 50 years in the accounts, may have increased significantly in value. The real open market value of the computer will therefore be significantly less than the book value and the property significantly more.

Because the book value of assets in your balance sheet is based on their purchase price, there will also be some significant 'assets' of the company which may have no book value attributed to them at all. Do your brands, patents, trademarks, designs, copyright, customer list, contracts, employees, have a value? You would probably assume that they do, but they will not generally have a book value in your balance sheet.

Some businesses require very few physical assets, the real value lying in the people, contacts and know-how. Obviously in these types of businesses, the difference between the value of the business and the value of the net assets will be significant.

As a result of these problems with book valuation, businesses with reasonable performance will usually be expected to be sold for a value greatly in excess of the book value of the assets. The accounting term for the difference between the value of the assets and the value of the business is the **goodwill** of the business.

For these reasons, book values are hardly ever used for valuing a business although the price obtained for the business as a multiple of the book value is sometimes used as a cross check against similar calculations for other businesses in the same industry that have been recently sold to ensure that the price obtained is in line with those businesses.

Going concern value

This is a valuation of the assets of the business on the assumption that they are all to be sold together as a trading business. It therefore takes into account how much someone will be willing to pay for this collection of assets given the ability of the business to earn money. This is the type of valuation that, for example, a receiver will obtain for the assets of a business over which they have been appointed and which they hope to sell as a trading business or going concern.

The Royal Institute of Chartered Surveyors (RICS) sets out a standard for valuation known as **estimated realisation price** (ERP), also referred to as **open market value** or fair value, which is the price that might be expected to be achieved given a willing seller and a reasonable period within which to realise the property or other assets. This is the basis normally used for valuing property or plant and machinery, as part of a going concern valuation.

Forced sale value

Also known as a 'gone' valuation. This is the type of valuation that a liquidator would obtain when looking to sell the assets of a business that has ceased trading. It represents a breakup valuation of the assets so that there is no value to be obtained by their synergy as a package of assets with which to conduct a trade.

Obviously, your drop-dead price should never generally be significantly below the forced sale or break-up value of the assets unless your business has significant potential liabilities to take into account.

As before, the RICS publishes guidelines on preparation of a valuation called **estimated restricted realisation price** (ERRP) which is the value that a surveyor would expect to be able to obtain for property or plant and machinery given a restricted period (say six months for property, three months for plant and machinery) within which to sell.

Since both ERP and ERRP are used by different lenders to calculate the security value of assets against which they are prepared to lend to you, it is vitally important to understand on what basis the property or goods have been valued.

The main classes of items in the balance sheet and the general approach to valuation by purchasers are summarised below:

Asset	Valuation
Property; plant and machinery; finished goods stock	Professional valuation by chartered surveyor
Debtors	Review by corporate finance or insolvency accountant
Raw materials and work in progress	Professional valuation by a quantity surveyor
Liabilities	Accountant's review

MARKET VALUATION

This approach is somewhat akin to valuing a house for sale. To find a reasonable estimate for the value of your property, all you normally have to do is look in the property pages of local newspapers, find houses that are similar to yours, in a similar area, of similar size, work out the average price for a house with the same number of bedrooms, and then figure in an adjustment for the decorative state, potential, land, or any other special features your own property has.

Similarly, with many businesses, by looking at the trade press or by contacting professional valuers specialising in your type of business, you should be able to identify a number of businesses that have sold in your industry and the prices achieved in the recent past to allow you to judge the basis of valuation.

If you are an active member of a trade association you may actually be able to call and speak to a number of other business principals who have been involved in buying or selling businesses of your type and obtain information from them directly as to the basis of the valuation involved.

An alternative approach is to consider comparing your valuation to those of publicly traded businesses in your industry, on the basis of the ratio of their price (business value) to earnings (profits), or **P/E ratio**, as published in *The Financial Times* and other financial press. This approach should be treated with extra caution however as because these businesses are publicly traded, there is a ready market for their shares. People buying their shares in the public markets therefore have less risk because they know they are publicly traded and therefore if they decide that they no longer wish to hold the shares they are able to sell them. The shares therefore have 'liquidity'. Because there is not a public market in your shares, your business is unlikely to attract the sort of price earning multiples that a similar public company would.

If you wish to use a P/E ratio to consider business values, points to be careful of include:

- The earnings figure on which any calculation should be based should be the sustainable earnings figure, that is to say one that has been adjusted to remove some of the items described, but also needs to reflect the realistic prospects of the business.

- Ensure that you are comparing like with like as you will find that most P/E multiples published will be based on earnings after tax. Applying an after tax P/E ratio to a pretax earnings figure will obviously give you an inflated valuation.

- Most publicly quoted companies will be of a scale significantly different to a private company and again the scale of operation and perceived reduction in risk means that an investor is likely to accept a higher P/E ratio in a publicly quoted company than in a private one.

♦ Given the scale of publicly quoted companies, and therefore the diversity of their operations, it may be extremely difficult to find a quoted company that is sufficiently focused to truly provide an equivalent to your business.

♦ As has already been discussed, public companies are under pressure to manage their figures so as to show good earnings for their shareholders, whilst private companies are not motivated to maximise earnings, as this tends to result in tax that owners would rather not pay. Therefore the underlying approach to accounting policies, **gearing** and tax management may differ significantly between a private company and a public company in an equivalent industry, leading to significantly different earnings figures.

There has been some research done into the relative P/E ratios achieved from the sale of public and private companies. This tends to show that private companies obtain a P/E ratio roughly 50–60% of the equivalent public company P/E ratio.

When reviewing P/E ratios published in the financial press, you may well come across some that appear to be extremely high. You may, for example, wonder why anyone would buy a share with a P/E ratio of 75 or 100, when this indicates that they would have to hold the share, in effect, for 75 or 100 years to generate sufficient earnings to pay back the price of the share. The answer is that P/E ratios tend to be determined by the perceptions of a company's growth prospects. Therefore a publicly quoted company with a high P/E ratio is one where the market believes that it has high growth prospects and that investors are prepared to pay a high amount for shares now in the belief that the earnings will grow significantly in the near future so as to give a good return on their investment.

Given the numbers of assumptions that will have to be made in terms of determining an appropriate P/E multiple to use coming up with a valuation, for the reasons given above, a P/E ratio approach to valuation is usually considered too subjective, particularly when compared with the discounted cashflow approach.

DISCOUNTED CASHFLOW

Discounted cashflow, also known as **net present value**, works on the following basis. Which would you prefer, £1 now or £1 in a year's time?

If you are rational, you would prefer £1 now, because not only is £1 in a year's time by definition more uncertain than £1 now (I might not be around to offer it or have changed my mind), but £1 in a year's time is actually worth less than £1 now because you could place the pound I give you now in a bank account and earn interest on it for a year. In fact, if you could obtain a 10% net rate of interest, then in theory £1 now is equivalent to a minimum of £1.10 in a year's time. Similarly you can see that £1.10 in a year's time, given that rate of available interest, is the equivalent discounted back to a present value of £1.

Discounted future cashflows are therefore used as a way of estimating what somebody is prepared to pay now, for the future stream of cash that is going to be generated by having bought a particular asset, business or project. The discounting of anticipated future cashflows is the method used in most large corporate transactions for business valuations for the purposes of mergers, acquisitions and disposals. For the purpose of valuing businesses, a theory called the capital asset pricing model generates a discount rate based on the 'risk free' rate of interest that someone requires for investing their money rather than spending it (which is equivalent to the rate of return they would get by putting their money into, say, government stocks), times a risk factor for investing in a particular sector, known as beta which is generated by looking at returns generated by quoted companies.

For smaller businesses it is more appropriate to use the weighted average cost of capital or WACC. A simple example of how this is calculated is shown in Figure 4 for a company that is funded by £50,000 worth of long-term loans and £100,000 worth of share capital where loans have an interest rate of 10% per annum and the equity is rewarded by a dividend rate of 20% per annum.

	Capital	Cost as %	Cost of capital
	£000	%	£
Equity (share capital)	100	20	20
Debt (long-term loans)	50	10	5
	150		25 = 16.66% weighted average cost of capital

Figure 4. Weighted average cost of capital.

Under the discounted cashflow approach to valuation, the value of your business to an acquirer is the total of the future discounted net cashflows after tax. A simplistic example of a discounted cashflow covering three years is set out in Figure 5.

	Year 1	Year 2	Year 3
Operating profit	100	120	140
Add back depreciation	10	20	20
'Cash profit' generated from trading	110	140	160
Movement in working capital	10	(5)	15
Capital expenditure		(100)	
Tax payment	(33)	(40)	(40)
Net post tax cashflow	87	(5)	135
Discount rate compound 10% pa	1.1%	1.21%	1.33%
Cashflow discounted to present values	79.1	(4.1)	101.5
Total present value	176.5		
Price paid	(150.0)		
Net present value	26.5		

Notes:
- No residual value after year 3
- Discount from year 1

Figure 5. Example of discounted cashflow.

Thus the net cashflows generated by the prospect of £227 (£87 + £135 − £5) are equivalent to £176.5 now when discounted back to present values. Deducting the £150 that you have to pay to acquire these cashflows therefore gives a net present value of £26.5.

The disadvantages of the discounted cashflow technique are:

- The appropriate discount rate for the valuation will be the purchaser's weighted average cost of capital, or the discount rate the purchaser wishes to apply to a business with your risk profile. Obviously this figure will vary from purchaser to purchaser and therefore you will have to make an assumption as to what the purchaser's appropriate discount rate will be to calculate a discounted value.

♦ For how many years going forward should you calculate a discounted value before inserting a residual value that represents the entire future value of the business from that point to infinity?

♦ To what extent is a purchaser prepared to pay for the benefits in increased operational efficiencies, synergies etc that will come about from their purchase of the business? How far should these be stripped out of any projections?

Nevertheless there are many advantages to using a discounted cashflow approach in that it forces a rigorous and quantified examination of a variety of issues that will be relevant to the performance of the business going forwards such as:

♦ Any expected movement in profitability (up or down) whether for reasons already inherent in the business or from factors that come into play as a result of the sale to the new party.

♦ The profitability of individual areas of the business which may vary significantly from business unit to business unit.

♦ Capital expenditure required to develop the business or the scope to realise capital repayments by way of future disposal of parts of the business by the acquirer.

♦ Any increases required in working capital to cope with growth and turnover, or any reduction of working capital that might be achieved by way of better financial management following the sale.

♦ Any other synergies or changes arising from the acquisition such as changes in the accounting date which impact upon the due date for taxation payments.

Whilst it may appear complex, discounted cashflow forecasting approaches lend themselves well to spreadsheet applications and, once set up, the key assumptions can be varied and revised forecasts run off with ease.

It is however easy to become confused as to which forecast was based on which set of assumptions, so ensuring strict rules about 'version control' and fully annotating the assumptions that lie behind each alternative forecast are vital so as to minimise confusion.

Such models can also be easily flexed to reflect changes in assumptions (so what if sales are 10% better than forecast, or 10% worse than forecast?) to see how these affect the outcome. This process is known as 'sensitivity analysis' as you are looking to see how sensitive the outcome is to changes in key assumptions.

Discounted cashflows are also used to calculate the **internal rate of return** (IRR) of the project. The IRR is the percentage discount rate at which the net present value of the interest is zero. For the case above it is 18.88%. This means that the project overall gives a return of 18.88% as shown below.

	Year 1	Year 2	Year 3
Net post tax cashflow	87.0	(5.0)	135.0
Discount rate compound 25.15%	1.1888	1.4132	1.680
Cashflow discounted to present value	73.2	(3.5)	80.4
Total present value	150.0		
Price paid	(150.0)		
Net present value	0.0		

From the point of view of the finance director of a purchasing company, the decision whether they should buy or not in practice comes down to which is higher, WACC or the IRR as:

♦ if our weighted average cost of capital is 10%

♦ and the return on the investment (ie the IRR) of this purchase is 20%

♦ then it makes sense to employ our capital/borrow funds and pay out WACC of 10%, to invest and make 20%.

RETURN ON INVESTMENT

If the purchaser is looking to buy your business, they are presumably doing so on the assumption that it will make profits into the future which will provide them with a return on their investment. In addition to IRR above, this return can be expressed as a simple percentage such that if a purchaser buys your business for £1 million, and expects it to generate earnings (ie profits) of say £200,000 in the year after acquisition, as a crude measure, the return on their investment is £200,000 ÷ £1 million = 20%.

Obviously the above does not take into account the cash implications of the deal on their existing business (such as capital expenditure, movement in working capital etc), in the way that discounted cashflows and therefore IRR does. It is therefore a more crude measure. However, extending the principle gives other indicators which investors may use to consider the value of the business.

The second of these is **payback period**, which is again a crude way of measuring risk. In this case, assuming that earnings will continue to run at £200,000 per year, the payback period (ie the period it will take until the original investment has been paid back) is £1 million ÷ £200,000 or five years. Obviously the shorter the payback period, the quicker the purchaser will be 'seeing their money back'.

The same formula (£1 million ÷ £200,000) also gives the P/E ratio referred to above.

SECTOR SPECIFIC

Many trades, particularly those where there are a relatively large number of small businesses with therefore a constant high number of such business sales during any one business year, tend to develop their own specific basis of valuation and normal deal structure.

For example, you will often see a professional firm, such as solicitors or accountants, sold on the basis of a multiple or gross recurring fees, while valuation of a hotel will be a function of room rate, occupancy rate, and number of rooms; restaurant valuations will be driven by numbers of covers; and pubs by barrelage.

Brokers in these areas of business will often express a valuation in terms of these key metrics. So, for example, brokers dealing with residential care homes will often express a value in terms of £X per bed, for comparison purposes.

As a result, fairly standard bases of sales valuation may grow up such as: 'For business type X, the sale value is likely to be twice annual gross sales plus the stock, furniture and fittings at cost.'

In addition, there may also be fairly standard approaches to structuring a deal. This is particularly applicable to small service or professional businesses where the value of the business often lies in the personal contacts and network of the existing owner of the business. Any purchaser considering buying such a business has first of all to make an assessment as to whether there is a business once the principal has gone. Assuming that the purchaser believes they can manage the business once the principal has departed, they then have to consider to what extent the business's earnings will be damaged by the departure of the principal and how they can best manage this to reduce the damage. In these circumstances, a payment spread out over a period of years based on expected earnings, with the existing owner staying on as either an employee or a consultant for a period of say, one, two, or even three years in order to ensure a smooth handover of the business and the contact base to the new owner, and with an escalator either increasing the price paid if performance exceeds expectations or reducing it if it falls away, is not unusual.

EARNINGS MULTIPLES

The most commonly used basis of valuation, particularly for manufacturing businesses is the multiple of earnings approach. This is calculated simply on the basis of earnings/profits (before interest and tax, known as **EBIT** or **PBIT**) times the appropriate multiple. The level of multiple to be applied is then obviously a matter of judgement, given the strength of the business and the current economic circumstances, but it would not be unreasonable to expect a multiple of say five to seven times current earnings, when looking to sell an established manufacturing business with a good market position, albeit subject to normal competitive pressures that requires involvement of a good management team.

The worse the competitive position or reliance on strong management, the lower the multiple that should be expected. The clearer the competitive advantage and steadiness of the earnings stream, the higher the multiple that would be sought.

WHAT PURCHASERS WILL AND WILL NOT PAY FOR

It is evident from the above that earnings, both current and future, are crucial to almost every business valuation whether in terms of profit or cash. So earnings, current and future, are the starting point for a purchaser and a seller to consider valuation. This therefore reinforces the point that the seller needs to be able to demonstrate the business's real earnings potential, by pointing to demonstrable profits and earnings in the business. This means that the seller needs to be thinking ahead and ensuring that all earnings and profits are clearly and demonstrably flowing through the business's books so as to be able to show these to a purchaser when the time comes.

If you have been diverting profit or business off into another vehicle, or into personal trading or doing work in the black economy, do not expect to be able to persuade the purchaser to rely on your word that such earnings exist and should be taken into account when they calculate how much they are prepared to pay for your business!

Furthermore, do not expect the purchaser to pay for the benefits they will bring to the business. If your business is turning over £1 million and making £100,000 profit, you may feel that once this has been acquired by Large Co, because of their extensive distribution network and manufacturing expertise they should be able to grow your business to sales of £3 million and profits of £450,000 within a couple of years. This may be completely correct, however, do not base your idea of the business's value on a turnover of £3 million and profits of £450,000, because the purchaser will be taking the view that value will only arise as a result of the work they have to do on your business once they have acquired it, and they will not base their purchase valuation on this future worth following their input, but upon its current performance.

Finally, remember also that turnover as such does not have a value. Turnover is only a tool to generate profit and it is the profit that your business generates as a return on the investment in buying it that will have a value for a purchaser.

Do not expect purchasers to factor into their prospective offer prices any element of 'compensation' to you for either the emotional effects of giving up your business, or the costs and time you have put into building the business to where it is today. The brutal truth is that the purchaser is not interested in how much time or money you have spent on developing your business. They will be interested in how much money they can earn from running the business going forwards in respect of which your sunk costs are completely irrelevant.

SUMMARY

The business's value is what somebody is prepared to pay for it; and what they are prepared to pay for generally is a future stream of profits and cash. The only question therefore is how much money are they prepared to pay for that future income given its apparent degree of risk or reliability?

In summary the basic methods of valuation and their pros and cons are as follows:

	Pro	Con
Asset value: the value of all the assets, less the value of liabilities on either a 'book' or a professionally valued basis	Going concern and forced sale values provide 'cover' against worst case	Book values are 'meaningless' and asset valuations do not reflect value of the trading business being bought
Market value: the going rates for your type of business	Easily understood comparison	Difficulty of getting the relevant reliable, comparable information
Discounted cashflow: the value of your future annual cashflows, discounted back to the present value in terms of cash today	Makes everything explicit and qualified	Finding the correct discount rate and the underlying uncertainty of future cashflows
Return on investment: the profit earned in future years expressed as a percentage of the investment required	Easy comparison between investment opportunities	Not cash based and dependent on projection of future earnings
Sector specific: standard basis used for your particular trade	Common basis for comparison	Do not reflect the individual circumstances of the business and its properties
Multiple of earnings: profits times a 'multiple'	Subjective but readily understood	Not cash based and relies on a projection of future earnings

5

Making the Business Attractive

GROOMING FOR SALE

Grooming is the term for the process of preparing a business for sale and making it as attractive as possible to prospective purchasers. To properly groom a business for sale may take two or three years, although if you haven't got that long it is still worth taking whatever steps you can to groom the business as these will pay off and a higher price will be achieved.

The main areas to consider on preparing a business for sale are:

- profiling the profits
- polishing the plant
- preparing the paperwork
- providing peace of mind.

PROFILING THE PROFITS

As has been discussed, a purchaser is principally going to be interested in knowing how much profit the business may be expected to make going forwards, as they are essentially buying that future stream of profits (and cash).

Set out below are the recent profit profiles of four companies, each of which in the last year generated a profit of £50,000, together with a purchaser's likely reaction to the profile shown.

Company A: No evidence of growth. Performance is likely to remain flat going forwards.

A purchaser would make no assumption or allowance for growth in coming up with a purchase price for Company A.

Company B: Has had a high rate of growth, but growth has peaked – is the industry heading for a shakeout or contraction?

With Company B, the purchaser might actually assume that profits are likely to fall in the near future, as a result of an industry shakeout.

Company C: Profits are wildly variable. Is the next move up or down?

Whilst Company C can make extremely good profits, it also has the risk of making extremely poor ones, and a purchaser would discount the multiple they would apply to profits to reflect this fact.

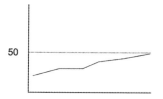

Company D: Strong, steady, reliable track record of growth. Is there any reason it won't continue to grow?

Company D shows a strong, steady growth in profits over a number of years and, unless there is some major shock in the wings, the purchaser would take comfort from this strong track record when projecting forwards future expected earnings.

Therefore to achieve the best sales price for your business, your profit and growth track record should look as much like Company D's as possible.

There are also a number of areas in respect of finance that will need attention in the years prior to a sale, both in order to be able to demonstrate the actual profitability of the business and also in order to make the sale as easy as possible. The key areas for action are summarised below.

Have your accounts audited

Even if your business is exempt from producing audited accounts, consider having your accounts audited from this point forwards.

In a strict legal sense, your purchaser will not be able to rely on the audited accounts, since the accountant's opinion is not actually addressed to them and they would have significant difficulty in holding the auditors to account for their report. In addition, since the purchaser will be conducting their own due diligence using their own firm of accountants to audit your results and your status, why should you bother with the expense of obtaining audited accounts?

Accounts, however, that have been audited carry a significantly higher level of credibility than unaudited ones. They therefore help to demonstrate your confidence in your business's performance and its systems for recording its performance, as well as providing comfort for the purchaser and that the numbers upon which they are basing their decision have some basis in reality.

Operate ethically

Following on from using professional advisors to audit your accounts, if you are engaged in any special arrangements designed in order to avoid paying tax you should stop immediately for a number of reasons. If you want an audit opinion, you want a clean audit opinion, not one that is qualified over disputes on revenue recognition or failure of your accounting systems to record all the company's business.

Remember that when considering what to pay for the business, the buyer will be looking at the recognisable underlying profits of the business. When considering what to pay for a stream of income, the buyer will only really recognise easily traceable and easily reconstructable profits. Would you pay a multiple of six times earnings for earnings that could not be seen in the books of accounts of the business you are buying? The buyer will not want to pay a multiple of profits that are not easily and clearly demonstrable.

Diversion of earnings in order to save tax therefore has two adverse effects. First it depresses the price you are likely to achieve because if a buyer is paying a multiple of earnings they won't pay that multiple for things they cannot see. Secondly, you will depress the price or may even lose the sale altogether because the buyer will think they are buying from a crook. The buyer will have to factor that knowledge about your business ethics into their calculations about what multiple to pay, what risks they are running in purchasing the business from somebody with that attitude, what potential liabilities it may give rise to later (eg as a result of a subsequent tax investigation) and, indeed, whether to go ahead with the purchase at all, given the risks that all this may involve.

When looking at selling a business it pays to invest in paying taxes for a number of years, bearing in mind that if you achieve a sale at a multiple of six or seven times earnings, you will recover this money many times over on the eventual sale.

Rationalise the business

As they grow, many businesses acquire a variety of peripheral areas of activity arising out of, or related to, their core business. Some of these additional activities may be significant contributors to profit, others may be more marginal. In the sale of your business, you will be looking to demonstrate clear profitability. If your business has a large variety of peripheral or add-on areas of activity that confuse the picture, this may not help you in being able to show a purchaser the clear strong performance of the core business you wish to demonstrate.

Therefore, a number of years before looking for a sale, take a step back and review your business. Identify its core business and assess how strong, profit-making and cohesive a group they are. Review carefully all the ancillary, marginal or non-core activities. Those that have a clear market position and strong profitability you may well wish to keep in order to bolster the profitability of the core business. Those that simply confuse the picture, or give poor returns, you should either turn around or dispose of in advance of your main sale so as to be able to show a clear, easy to understand picture of a well focused business with strong central profits.

Clean the balance sheet

In addition to a clear picture of profits, you also need to be able to provide a clear picture of the balance sheet. Therefore a part of the preparation for sale involves cleaning up the balance sheet. The longer term issues involve identifying company assets (such as land and buildings) which you wish to remove from the company prior to the sale.

In the medium term, you need to review liabilities which may cause problems to a purchaser's due diligence. Specific issues tend to be shareholder loans which complicate the picture and which, where possible, should be paid back prior to going in to a sales process; and intercompany trading accounts which the purchaser will need to review in detail in order to see what the true asset and liability position is of each business as a standalone entity, together with identifying whether the turnover and profitability of any of the businesses has been artificially inflated by means of intercompany trading.

Clean the current assets

Finally, in the short term, before going into a sale, review your stocks and purchase and sales ledger (aged creditors and aged debtors). Where there are old or doubtful debts or slow moving items of stock, these should be written off. There are two reasons for this. First when your purchaser's accountants go through their due diligence process, they like to pick up these items anyway and they will be used against you in order to negotiate down the purchase price. Secondly, by recognising them now, prior to a sale, you can actually get value out of them, because as specific write-offs they should be allowable for tax and will therefore minimise your tax liability in the year coming up to sale.

GOLDEN RULE 9

Start early when grooming for sale

Allow yourself plenty of time to manage the business's profits so as to be able to clearly demonstrate proof of strong and growing profits.

POLISHING THE PLANT

The way your factory, offices, plant, equipment and stock are kept will make a significant impression on purchasers when they first visit your premises, not only about the plant and equipment itself, but also about how efficiently the business is operated and how reliable the controls are likely to be.

If you visit a plant that looks a complete shambles, this does not inspire confidence in that company's accounts, or in the accuracy of the costing information you will receive.

If you visit a company where the production environment is spic and span, the machines look well tended and maintained, the flow of goods through the factory is orderly, and the stock looks well segregated and identified, you will start out by having more confidence that any accounting information about profits or costings has a better chance of being accurate.

And let's not forget, the purchaser's purchase price is likely to be based on a multiple of profits, and the multiple they are prepared to put on it is a measure in some degree of their confidence in both the underlying current profitability and the risks associated with future projections. You should be allowing nothing to happen in your business that has any possibility of undermining a prospective purchaser's confidence in the business or its figures at any time during the sales process.

The premises and plant and equipment should therefore be painted, and any repairs needed should be undertaken. Obsolete plant and equipment should be disposed of so that it does not clutter the place up. Stock should be quite clearly segregated into tidy and clearly identifiable spaces, with racking installed with clearly identified bay numbers for location of stock (that should then tie up to the stock records). Where stock or cartons have to be stacked, stacks should be neat and tidy and pallets or cartons should be arranged neatly in rows or at right angles to each other as this helps to give an impression of order. Any land around the factory should be tidy and well maintained. Recognise that the reception area sets the tone for people's expectations of the business and should therefore be fitted out and kept tidy and professional in appearance.

Go through the offices and ensure that filing is tidy and put away, loose papers are cleared up or disposed of.

It is not possible to overemphasise the difference in perceived value between visiting a plant that is clean and crisp in appearance as compared to one that is a mess.

You will also find that your employees will be much more productive in a business that is well organised and will make a favourable impact on the buyer.

Review the flow of work through the premises. Stock and raw materials should ideally come in at one end, follow a logical process through the production process sequences throughout the factory and exit at the other end as finished goods, straight out on to a lorry and out to the customer. If your processing involves a lot of moving goods from one station to another in no apparent logical order, consider reorganising the plant and equipment so that you do get a sensible workflow.

A particularly tricky issue during a prolonged presale grooming process is whether or not you should invest in upgrading plant and equipment or premises in the years leading up to a sale. Dependent on the business's circumstances, this can have a major impact on its value.

It is difficult to give a hard and fast rule as to whether you should undertake such projects or not. The downside is the degree of expenditure and cost that may not be reflected in increased value of the assets being sold. And if you are going to invest in major change, such as for example installing a new IT system, or relocating plant and equipment, in addition to the actual purchase cost, appreciate you may well also suffer further costs through disruption and upheaval in your existing business operations.

Against this must be set the potential writing down of the multiple that a prospective purchaser will apply to your business on the basis that its plant and equipment, systems, or premises are out of date and will require investment following the purchase.

If you do go ahead with a major investment or change, you must ensure that it is completed before you enter into the actual sale process. Stepping into the purchaser's shoes for a moment, who would want to buy a business that is in the middle of a major change in its operations, plant and equipment or systems, and suffering from all the associated disruption? Major projects are often the 'straws' that break the camel's back and that can lead to a business failure (see *Turning Your Business Around,* Mark Blayney) and the uncertainty and disruption associated with the business during a major change will lead a purchaser to discount what they are prepared to pay as a result of the extra risk this carries.

When contemplating whether to invest in new plant, equipment or systems, bear in mind that your business has not been sold until it has actually been sold. Therefore I recommend continuing to trade your business throughout the period leading up to and through a sale as though the sale were not going to take place. On this argument, if it makes sense for your business to invest in items of plant, machinery, equipment, or a new IT system, then that is what you should do, irrespective of the fact that you may at the same time be contemplating selling. Consult with your advisors during your sale planning and if you do invest comfort yourself with the idea that it will help you to negotiate a good price for your business when you do come to sell, since your investment is there to protect the future earnings of the business and therefore reduces the risk and increases the multiple that the purchaser ought to be willing to pay you for the business.

GOLDEN RULE 10

Tidy up the physical plant

Don't forget that first impressions count. If you put yourself in the buyer's shoes and were to visit your premises today for the first time with the thought 'Should I buy this business?' how impressed would you be? Does your plant look tidy, with everything in its place and work flowing through well maintained machines efficiently and in a controlled manner? Or is it chaotic, stock looking untidy, machines looking in need of a lick of paint or maintenance?

PREPARING THE PAPERWORK

The sorts of items that will be reviewed by the purchaser's advisors during due diligence are covered in Chapters 10 and 11 while typical checklists of financial and legal documents to be requested from a company being sold are given in Chapter 10. Since you want the sale to go ahead as smoothly as possible with the minimum of surprises and ammunition for the purchaser to reduce their offer price as a result of items found during due diligence, the first thing to do is to ensure that all your books and records are tidy and up to date.

Given the variety of areas that are looked at under a due diligence, you need to interpret books and records very widely to include not only your accounting records and your regular management accounts, profit and loss, balance sheet, cashflow forecasts, and aged debtor and creditor lists, but also your payroll and tax record and your company secretarial records such as register of charges, minute book and share register.

In addition to these, there are then a variety of operational and commercial matters which need to be kept up to date, such as files on banking arrangements and facilities in place; any distribution or licensing agreements; your trademarks, copyright, patents, and other intellectual property; and your commercial agreements, such as leases or contracts.

You should use the checklists in Chapter 10 to review this area well in advance of the sales process to give yourself time to resolve any problems discovered.

You should also ensure that all items which need to be codified into contracts have been. Check to ensure that you have contracts of employment for your employees and your directors and put together a file containing copies of the lease for your premises, and leases on all key items of plant and equipment.

As the purchaser is broadly interested in the future underlying profits of the business, the more certain the future results are the better you are able to justify a higher multiple. One way of attempting to improve certainty is by reducing the risk of specific changes, for example a purchaser may be extremely concerned that relationships with a group of customers or suppliers are dependent upon your personal contact with them over a number of years and the risk that these relationships may not be reliable once you have sold the business. This concern may then cause the purchaser to reduce the multiple they are prepared to pay for it. One way to try to reduce this apparent risk to the purchaser is by turning such relationships with customers or suppliers, wherever possible, into contractual agreements.

By doing so you can argue to the purchaser that you have reduced the purchaser's reliance on simple goodwill and relationships and replaced this with a legal contractual relationship on which the purchaser can rely.

Whether a relationship has been codified into a contract or not, you will need to give careful thought, again as part of the grooming for sale process, as to how relationships are to be managed during transition to the new owners.

At the same time, review your existing key contracts and identify any that will expire shortly after your proposed sale. Consider renegotiating any such contracts so that at the time of the sale the purchaser will have the certainty of the contract going forwards for a number of years. Again, by reducing this uncertainty you will reduce their perceived risk as to the sustainability of the projected profits and thereby help to improve the multiple obtained.

Check to ensure you have not entered into any commitments that would actively prevent you from selling. Some soft loans (for example a loan from a brewery to refurbish a pub or nightclub) may come with a condition that the owner does not sell the business for a specified period, so that the brewery can ensure it gains the full advantage that is expected from having made the loan. Similar conditions might be attached to grants, where on the event of the sale of the business to owners within a specified period, the grant is repayable.

Landlords

Where the ownership of a business is going to change, for example a sale of the business and assets of Company A to a purchaser Company B, or the sale of a business by individual Mr A to Company B, the position of the landlords is vital as they often have the power to kill deals. They therefore need to be involved in the process early enough.

In theory almost all property leases are transferable to a new owner (assignable) as they will generally include a clause allowing assignment. This clause is usually qualified in that the landlord has to provide consent to the sale although this consent should not be unreasonably withheld.

So what is reasonable or unreasonable in these circumstances? Well, when granting a lease to a tenant a landlord will undertake a variety of credit checks to ensure that the tenant is likely to be able to pay the rent whilst in occupation. If the tenant then decides to sell the lease on to another prospective tenant, the landlord will want to ensure that the new tenant is at least as able to pay the rent as the old tenant. A tenant's perceived financial strength and ability to pay the rent is known as its 'covenant'. A prospective tenant who is clearly financially strong and able to pay the rent going forwards is a strong covenant; a tenant where there may be significant doubts about the strength of their cashflow and therefore their ability to pay the rent is a weak covenant.

In looking at a proposed transfer of ownership from the existing tenant to a new tenant, the landlord will be looking to ensure that they are not weakening the covenant in relation to the premises.

Similar considerations to those of landlords will apply to a range of franchise businesses, tied distributors of certain products (such as car main dealers) or users of licensed trademarks or brand names.

PROVIDING PEACE OF MIND

When looking to groom your business for sale, try to put yourself into the prospective purchaser's shoes. Looking at your business from the buyer's point of view, if you were thinking about buying your business, what aspects of it would worry you the most? There is a very natural human tendency to look at the strengths and weaknesses of your operation and spend time polishing the strengths. But when a purchaser is coming along to look at your business, what they are most worried about are the risks that arise out of the weaknesses. Therefore, you need to consider your business critically to identify the weakest parts of it for most concerted action.

Accounting systems

Bearing in mind that your purchaser will bring in a team of accountants to undertake the due diligence process, first and foremost you need to be able to demonstrate that you have adequate financial systems and controls in place. After all, these will be accountants reviewing your business, so what do you think they will want to ensure they have covered properly?

However, this is not just a case of professional pride. The buyer will need to feel comfortable that you operated and are still operating good financial systems as, in making a judgement as to what multiple to apply to earnings, they need to be confident that not only is the existing earnings figure broadly correct but that they can understand what is going on so as to adequately be able to judge the strengths or weaknesses of existing and projected income. The buyer will need to be confident that they understand all the business's liabilities and that these are all recorded in the company's books and have been recognised as a cost. They will also need to be sure that stock has been correctly quantified and costed and that prices quoted on contracts have been calculated on a sensible basis so as to make a profit. Each of these areas relies on an efficient accounting system.

Management team

The purchaser will also be aware that in order to deliver the projected income they need management in place who are able to manage the business to obtain the results. So, particularly where you are looking to retire as part of the sale, a vital part of grooming the business for sale is building an adequate management team who we tied into the business and will be able to carry on once you have left and to put in place management and information systems that capture your specialised knowledge so that this is clearly in place for the purchaser going forwards.

Again, what the buyer will be looking for is comfort that current earnings will lead through to projected future earnings. This implies a high degree of continuity between the trends before and after the sale which can only really be delivered if there is a strong management team committed to the business and which transfers across with the business on sale. If you are building a business that is completely dependent upon you, your skills, your contacts, and your management of the business, without a management team that could survive without you, you are not building a saleable business, you are running a one-man band that will not survive you. A business run by an owner with a team of managers in place who are anxious, willing and able to take the business forward is much more attractive to a prospective purchaser.

Outstanding practical issues

As part of the commercial due diligence, the purchaser will want to look at a range of operational and commercial issues. So now is the time to look hard at all the operational issues in your business, such as rate of customer returns, complaints and credit notes required, quality problems, and scrap rates so that when the purchaser's accountants come to review these statistics, they will all be at acceptable levels.

Environmental risks

Finally, you should not forget environmental issues when grooming your business for sale.

The potential costs of environmental issues have driven this item up in purchasers' concerns over the last few years. You will find that many buyers are likely to ask for warranties in respect of environmental issues, so it is good practice to have an environmental audit done well in advance so that any issues arising can be resolved by you in advance of any due diligence undertaken by the prospective purchaser. Alternatively you can then have a second environmental audit done to demonstrate the problems have been dealt with.

Whilst on the subject of these types of external audits, where appropriate you should maintain records of external insurance, fire safety, and health and safety reviews, and the actions taken to respond to any points raised, as these may also be looked at as part of a due diligence exercise.

GOLDEN RULE 11

Once you've got it looking good, keep it looking good.

As you go through the sales process remember that until you have actually sold the business it is not sold. So don't let either your operations or the way you are presenting your plant and equipment slip as you go through the process. Keep the business looking attractive, keep the hours being worked normal, keep the stock at the appropriate levels, right up until the time when you have signed on the dotted line and collected the cash.

THE ADVANTAGES OF BEING WELL GROOMED

Grooming performs two vital functions. First it is designed to make your business as interesting and as attractive to a prospective purchaser as possible, so as to ensure they make the best offer possible for the business and are as keen as possible to buy it. Secondly, combined with a 'mock due diligence' exercise, it is designed to ensure that the sales process thereafter, including the due diligence carried out by the purchaser's advisors, goes as smoothly as possible, gives rise to as few hitches as possible, and certainly gives rise to no unpleasant surprises or grounds on which the purchaser can seek to negotiate the price downwards.

It is therefore designed to help support getting both the best price in the sale and the sale through as smoothly as possible.

Time invested in preparing the business for sale will repay itself many times over in a less risky and more rewarding sales process.

GOLDEN RULE 12

Avoid surprises

There is nothing that causes more problems in the sales process than an unexpected surprise discovered late in the day. Thorough prior preparation of your business, its leases, contracts, documents, title deeds and so on, helps prevent unnecessary surprises.

GOLDEN RULES SUMMARY

9. Start early when grooming for sale.
10. Tidy up the physical plant.
11. Once you've got it looking good, keep it looking good.
12. Avoid surprises.

6

Choosing Advisors

DO YOU NEED ADVISORS?

You are a successful businessperson. To have created a successful business you must know how to negotiate sales, and having built up a successful business in your own industry you must know the main players within it and who is likely to be interested in buying your business. Other than a solicitor to help with drawing up the final contract, why then do you need any costly professional advisors and what can they possibly add?

There is no doubt that professional advisors' fees are going to be expensive. While initial meetings with reputable advisors at which they discuss the prospective sales strategy will be free, almost all will then require some form of commitment fee usually amounting to several thousand pounds quite early on in the process. This is because most fee arrangements are based on a percentage of the total sales price achieved, typically ranging from say 2% to 5% of the sale price achieved, or on variations such as step percentages relating to achievement of specific target prices.

Such fees (known as contingent) are obviously uncertain and due to the length of the sales process can often take many months from the start of work to be received. The purpose of the commitment fee is firstly to ensure that the seller is a serious seller, so that the advisor does not spend a significant amount of time advising the client, preparing paperwork, and conducting marketing activities, only to find that the client fails to conclude a suitable transaction, and secondly, to cover some of the basic costs and overheads of undertaking such work.

Any commitment fee should in any event be treated as simply an advance against the total fee payable to the advisor on completion of the sale.

It is increasingly common for advisors to have minimum fee levels. The time taken in preparing the documentation and marketing for sale a £20m turnover business is probably much the same as marketing for sale a business turning over £2m, however the sales proceeds (assuming similar profit percentages apply), will obviously be significantly different as will all the resulting fees for the advisor.

Firms are therefore increasingly setting internal limits as to the minimum prospective fee level that they are prepared to accept an instruction on which to act (also known as a 'mandate'). At the time of writing, some of the larger corporate finance departments within the Big Four accountancy firms are rumoured to have minimum fee levels of between £150,000 and £200,000, some firms within the rest of the Top Ten accountancy firms have a guideline at between £50,000 to £60,000, whilst some practitioners within the rest of the Top 20 accountancy firms are starting to have guidelines of around the £20,000 to £30,000 mark.

Undoubtedly for many owners contemplating selling their business, such fees as a percentage of the likely sales proceeds will appear a large price to pay for advice. However, it is worth repeating that selling a business is a complex, long drawn out affair which will differ significantly from any other transaction with which you have been involved whilst trading and growing your business, and one which it is critical to get right. The potential cost of errors in dealing with the process of finding the buyer who is prepared to pay the most, negotiating the best price available, and structuring the most appropriate deal for your circumstances, before then managing the process of negotiation, due diligence, and completion through to a successful conclusion are so great, that they do generally outweigh the very real costs of getting good professional advice.

GOLDEN RULE 13

Get the best help available

Good professional advisors cost money. But good professional advice makes you more money than it costs. Selling your business is probably the most important single transaction you will ever undertake, do you really want to do it on the cheap? For a recommendation, email markb@reinventyourbusiness.co.uk

---

HOW DO YOU CHOOSE ADVISORS?

Given that good professional advice is so important to obtaining a good result, it is critical to get the best professional advisors working on your behalf and you will need the help of specialists in the area, not your current general business advisors.

You should therefore be looking for a number of qualities in your professional advisor, including:

- A high market reputation for doing successful deals. This demonstrates their professionalism and expertise and proves they can do the job. You are looking for somebody with a good track record who knows how to sell businesses for good money, you do not want somebody to be learning their trade or practising on your company because you need a good result. In addition, as we will come on to, part of the advisor's role is to put your business in front of prospective purchasers. Advisors with good track records of placing successful deals will have built up contacts with potential purchasers which means that your potential deal is likely to be looked at sooner and more seriously by prospective purchasers than if it is presented by someone with a poor or no reputation in the marketplace. You and your business will also be judged in part by the company you keep. Therefore if you engage an extremely professional, well known and successful advisor, you are demonstrating that you are someone who looks for and takes the best advice available. Put your business sale proceeds in the hands of a cowboy, and you will not impress prospective purchasers.

◆ The sales process will be a long, complex, and stressful one, so you need to look for someone with whom you will have a high degree of personal compatibility, whose views you will respect if you need to have difficult conversations about your business, the sales process, negotiations, or any changes that need to be made to how your business is run in order to obtain the maximum value. They will also need to demonstrate to you that they understand the objectives you are trying to achieve (which may range from the maximum cash from the sale and hang the consequences, through to securing the future of your long-term employees who you are leaving behind in the business) in how the sales process negotiations are managed.

◆ Since this personal compatibility is so important, you are also looking for evidence that the senior person with whom you are establishing this personal rapport is actually going to continue to provide you with the service you want and stay focused on achieving the sale of your business. You are therefore looking for some evidence that the business is not handling such huge numbers of business sales that it is obviously 'a numbers game' as far as they are concerned, since you want your business sale to have a focused level of attention. So you want to ensure that your specific advisor will not be working on so many deals that they will not be able to give your business the attention that you require with the result that you find much of the work on your sale is being handled by significantly more junior staff with less experience who you have not met during the tendering process. Inevitably, the advisor you deal with at say partner level, will be there principally to give advice and help you in discussion of your strategy and negotiation, while much of the legwork in terms of preparing documentation and undertaking activities such as market research will be done by a more junior manager within the firm so ensure that they have sufficient staff to handle the work involved in the deal as well as a sufficient range of expertise in all the areas required such as tax or pensions. You should also ensure you meet the whole of the team who will be working on your account, and ensure that you know and are comfortable with who is going to be doing what on your behalf.

HOW DO YOU FIND PROFESSIONAL ADVISORS?

Professional advisors, for the purposes of this chapter, are broadly accountants who are acting to sell your business. They will generally describe themselves as being corporate finance advisors or occasionally brokers. Their job in part is to help by project managing the sale and in this process they will assist you and other professional advisors who may need to be engaged, such as valuers.

In addition, you will undoubtedly need a good corporate finance solicitor to deal with negotiation of the sales contract. Again, just as marketing your business for sale and dealing with due diligence are specialist areas in accountancy, negotiating the details of the sales contract and the impact of warranties, escrow clauses and non-competition covenants are specialist legal areas where it pays to get the best advice. Many of the comments in this chapter concerning advisors will also apply to engaging your legal advisors.

Corporate finance advisors will generally be found in the corporate finance department of any accountancy firm of any size. This is also an area, however, where successful individuals within firms will often spin out to go on their own, setting up successful one, two or three partner 'boutiques' focusing on this area.

Other than as an indication of potential minimum fees, size of firm is therefore not necessarily any guarantee of the quality of service you will receive. Indeed, given the comments above about the need for personal attention and the focus by your professional advisors, there is potentially an argument that smaller may be better.

At the larger end, the main competition to the larger accountancy firms in business sales starts to come from merchant banks who also have their own 'mergers and acquisitions' (M&A) departments.

Finally, since business sales often form part of business turnaround or rescue processes, a number of individuals practising as company doctors are also successfully involved in the process of buying and selling businesses. If you are looking to sell your business and it is in some form of distress or difficulty, it may well be worth contacting one of these specialists (log on to the local help form at www.turnaroundhelp.co.uk for a referral).

So how to find the right advisor for you? There are a number of ways to identify potential corporate finance advisors.

Far and away the best is by way of personal recommendation. Contact your usual personal network of contacts within your industry or area to identify people who have sold their businesses over the past few years. Call them to find out who they saw, who they used and why, and how they performed. If you would like my suggestions for a local specialist, please contact me at markb@reinventyourbusiness.co.uk.

You may obtain professional recommendation to a local advisor through either your own accountant, or bank manager. Such recommendations can be extremely valuable as the introducer may well have had dealings with the advisor in the past, and therefore seen evidence of their abilities and work. You should however treat such recommendations with a certain degree of caution as most professionals, advisors and bankers operate in a local context of mutual work referral. For example, if your corporate bank manager has a target of 12 new accounts to open this year, he will be looking for accountants who can introduce him to sufficient numbers of new businesses that he can pitch and obtain work. At the same time, accountants will be looking to bank managers for introductions into new audit clients, and transactions such as business sales to generate their fees. There is therefore a significant trade of mutual leads between accountants, solicitors and bankers (known as 'reciprocity') where introductions are currency to be paid, received or banked.

When taking a recommendation from a professional advisor, you should therefore quiz them as to how much business they do or have done in the past with the person they are advising, and use the opportunity of having the recommendation to ask for referral sites to speak to as part of the process of following up with the suggested advisor.

I am not suggesting that your advisor or bank manager will introduce you to someone who will not be able to service your needs, as undoubtedly your advisor or bank manager will be looking for the firm they have introduced to do a good job so as to retain your business and goodwill into the future (particularly once you have come in to the money from the sale). You would therefore expect it to be in their best interests to introduce you to an effective and efficient player. Nevertheless you must bear in mind that they will have some self-interest in respect of their own business links with that individual.

To obtain a large list of individuals engaged in corporate finance activity, you can start by looking for information published by the regulatory bodies. The Institute of Chartered Accountants in England and Wales, for example, has a corporate finance faculty which many individuals in this area will have joined. The disadvantages of these sorts of list are however that there are a number of individuals of whom I am aware who are members of the faculty who are not involved in the buying and selling of businesses at all, either because their main area of activity is in another area (such as say, insolvency) or because within corporate finance they are more involved with other activities such as raising funds, floating businesses or debt restructuring. In addition, such lists do not give a full picture of all individuals practising as corporate finance advisors as some may belong to one of the other professional bodies in the UK for such individuals, such as the Institute of Chartered Accountants in Scotland or the Association of Certified Accountants. Finally, inclusion on such a list tells you nothing about an individual's track record and performance, which is obviously the vital element.

Another research based approach is to find a list of corporate finance work done within your area over the past few years and establish who the advisors were. Whilst there is at least one professional database available in the market which provides such details, this is probably not a practical option for the individual business owner seeking this type of information. However, regional business publications aimed at the mid corporate market (turnover say £5m to £50m) will often provide an annual or perhaps biannual list of deals done in the region as part of the information they provide to their readers. A trip to your local library to research such business magazines may assist you in identifying the appropriate advisors in your area.

If you do not choose an advisor based on strong personal recommendation, you may seek to have a presentation by a shortlist, of say two or three, to pitch for your business (a 'beauty parade'). Before engaging advisors via such a beauty parade you should also always seek and take up references in respect of prior work.

INSTRUCTING ADVISORS

In order to instruct professional advisors you will have to sign a letter of engagement. This is your formal contract with your advisors and your authority for them to act on your behalf.

You should review this carefully before signing as it covers such contractual matters as:

◆ The basis of their fees, including how they are to be calculated, and payment terms.

◆ Limitation of liability, where your advisor will seek agreement as to their maximum liability in the event of any problem arising as a result of their advice (and you should check their professional indemnity insurance cover).

The engagement letter should specify the scope of the work to be undertaken for the fees agreed, indicate what information you are expected to be able to prepare and supply for the purposes of the sale, and give the basis on which any further fees may be payable by you in respect of any other work needed which is not covered by the description and scope of the assignment.

Corporate finance professionals will generally seek an exclusive engagement to sell your business for a specified period. Ensure that when reviewing the letter of engagement you are clear as to whether or not fees are due to the advisor in the event that a buyer they introduce during their engagement period purchases the business after the expiry of their exclusivity period, and whether a fee is due to the advisor should you find a purchaser from another source during the period within which the advisor has been engaged.

However, once you have engaged your professional advisors and have signed up to paying their fees, it is important that you commit to working with them so that together you can seek to achieve the best deal for both sides. It will be a long and involved process and there needs to be a high degree of mutual trust. Occasionally sellers will attempt to pull a fast one on their professional advisors by seeking to deal direct with prospective purchasers and cut out their engaged professional advisors from the process. All I would say on this is that achieving a sale of your business is a difficult enough process in the first place, without adding to the stress and purchasers' enquiries by adding on a dispute with a firm of professional advisors into the process.

The letter of engagement should also make clear that the advisor is acting as your agent in any discussion or negotiation, and is empowered to undertake negotiations on your behalf with prospective purchasers.

The letter of engagement should also give assurances to you of the confidentiality of any information you provide to the advisor; the basis under which they are empowered to disclose this information to prospective interested parties. It should also act to safeguard your right to any of your intellectual property or know-how to which you give the agent access.

HOW DO YOU USE YOUR PROFESSIONAL ADVISOR?

You will use your professional advisor to undertake a number of specific functions in relation to the sales process, but also to provide a variety of skills and resources that are probably not available to you within your business as it stands.

The specific tasks that the advisor will undertake on your behalf can be reasonably simply listed. They include advising on the range of values of your business and helping you to clearly set out your personal objectives in undertaking the sale. From that they can help you develop the selling strategy and undertake the necessary research to produce a list of potential buyers, as well as producing the necessary documentation of confidentiality letters, invitations to tender and a **sales pack**.

Having discussed the approach with you, they can then undertake the marketing programme, contacting potential buyers, signing them up to the confidentiality agreement and arranging initial visits and discussions, managing the process through to the stage where serious negotiations can be conducted with a shortlist of seriously interested purchasers, until an acceptable offer and heads of agreement (or heads of terms) are achieved. Samples of some of the typical documentation involved are set out in Chapters 7, 8 and 9.

The advisor will then help to manage the progress of dealing with the purchaser's due diligence enquiries and supporting you and the solicitors in negotiation of the terms of sale so as to drive the sale through to a signed sales agreement. Thereafter they will also assist you in managing the closure process and handover such as dealing with preparation of completion accounts, and attendance at transaction stock counts.

Within all this, it is important to emphasise the project management role that your advisor needs to fulfil. A number of professionals will become involved in the sales process (your solicitors, the purchaser's solicitors, your valuers, their valuers, their due diligence team, the finance brokers, the purchaser's funders), and somebody needs to take responsibility for managing the timetable to push the deal through to conclusion. Your advisor is critical in this process (spurred on by their percentage of the final sales price achieved) in chasing outstanding issues and ensuring they are resolved so that a sale can be completed.

The skills, knowledge, and resources that your advisor therefore brings to the party and which are vital for completing the process include their experience, not only of the current market which is obviously relevant for both estimating values and managing the sales process, but also knowledge of the process itself (which problems are serious, which are trivial, what is holding something up, what can be done about it). They are also the overall guide on technical aspects such as tax, albeit that whilst able to give you general guidance they may need to act the role of ringmaster in bringing in specific experts to deal with detail issues (such as specific tax or pension planning enquiries), or professional valuers to look at the property.

Coming out of their knowledge of the marketplace is also knowledge of potential buyers outside the industry as well as access to them. Many business owners assume that the most likely purchaser for their business is somebody already in the industry. This may well be the case, however it is often also the case that the buyer who is prepared to pay the most is somebody from outside the industry who is looking to get in. A good professional advisor will have contacts across a wide variety of industries and should be able to spot such opportunities. In addition, because your advisor is continually involved in selling businesses, they will have ongoing dealings with a number of prospective purchasers of businesses and should therefore be able to get your proposal looked at with greater ease and seriousness than if you were to attempt to approach such purchasers directly.

These types of purchasers may include both other trading businesses looking to expand their position in your industry (a **trade sale**) and financial institutions, such as **venture capital (VC)** houses, looking to acquire businesses as investments (a **financial sale**).

As your advisor knows and deals with these purchasers on a regular basis, they know which sorts of deals will be of interest to which sort of purchaser. If you were to attempt to sell to a VC you might need to adopt a shotgun approach of contacting many in the hope of finding one who is interested in your type of activity or size of business. Your professional advisor, on the other hand, should be able to bring a more focused approach from their knowledge of who wants to do which deal and introduce your business to the two or three where there is a real chance of a deal being done. You should bear in mind that most professional purchasers of businesses are in effect continually bombarded with proposals and requests to invest in businesses. They look to professional advisors to filter these proposals and direct those which are worth their consideration to them. Professional advisors therefore build their credibility and their efficiency in managing sales by improving their ability to filter proposals, and only introduce them to the right parties. Again, introducing your sale to a prospective buyer through the right intermediary helps give it credibility and ensures it is looked at seriously.

Your professional advisor also provides a valuable barrier between you and the process of sale for much of the period. You may for example initially want to ensure you maintain confidentiality as to the fact that the business is for sale. This is obviously extremely difficult if you wish to act to sell the business yourself. By using a professional advisor however, the details of the business can be summarised under a code name and circulated to prospective interested parties so that you control the moment at which the real identity of the business is revealed to prospective purchasers. You can therefore screen potential buyers and ensure they are signed up to appropriate confidentiality agreements before providing them with detailed information. At the same time, while the sales process is continuing, having prospective purchasers deal mainly with the professional advisor has a number of advantages:

◆ It allows you to continue running the business, as opposed to getting bogged down in dealing with significant numbers of purchase enquiries or managing a mailshot programme and supply of sales packs.

◆ It allows somebody to continue to present the company in its best light and to act as an advocate and sales person for it without appearing to be emotionally involved and potentially egotistical (where there is a danger that you as the business owner and entrepreneur might actually put potential purchasers off by the way in which you sell the virtues of the business).

◆ It can significantly help in relation to managing negotiation of the price where your advisor acts as your agent in negotiating, but will be seen by the prospective purchaser as operating within a framework of a deal that you are seeking and your agent therefore always has the fallback of needing to check with you as principal before anything can be agreed. Your advisor should also be well practised in negotiating such business sales prices whilst bearing in mind the impact of proposals in respect of terms.

◆ Finally, it provides an important cut-out between you and the purchaser over any 'bad news' or disagreements over price, given that in many instances you will need to work with the purchaser following the sale for a period in relation to handing the business over. You would therefore want to avoid any highly emotionally charged disagreements or disputes during the price fixing process, which can be achieved by handling this through the use of a trained professional to negotiate this aspect.

GOLDEN RULES SUMMARY

13. Get the best help available.

7

How To Go About Selling Your Business

WHO WILL WANT TO BUY YOUR BUSINESS?

Prospective purchasers of your business either exist within it, in the form of family members, junior partners, or a prospective management **buy-out** team; or outside in the shape of a financial purchaser backing a management **buy-in** team, or a trade purchaser looking to acquire your business to add to their existing interests.

Since you already know the people within your business, this is usually the easiest place to start when looking to sell.

Selling to internal parties has a number of advantages in that they already know the nature of the business, its markets, customers, suppliers and so on, and therefore their need to go through an expensive fact finding exercise is significantly reduced (albeit not completely eliminated as they will need to undertake a fair amount of work in order to provide sufficient due diligence information for their financial backers).

In addition, you may be comfortable with negotiating structured payment terms or a buy-out over time by way of some form of earn-out or percentage royalties with such an internal team that you would not be comfortable with were you to be dealing with an external party. Additionally, even if you do not believe there is much prospect of a successful management buy-out, you may consider it worthwhile to explore the possibility with management, prior to going to a full sale process as, if your management feel they have had the chance to consider making a bid, but of themselves decided not to, this can reduce any chance of antagonism towards a successful external purchaser, which can help confirm to the purchaser that they have a committed and positive management team looking to take the business forward (as opposed to one harbouring resentment that they were not allowed to attempt an MBO, or worse, had one rejected). This is obviously a matter of judgement as to the personalities and nature of the internal management team, as undoubtedly in some circumstances it could also be counter productive (eg the fact that an internal management team did not pursue an MBO opportunity may colour the view of an external interested party).

Management buy-outs may or may not be undertaken backed by a venture capitalist (VC). In either circumstances they tend not to provide the best possible price in the marketplace and, if not backed by a financial institution, will generally require a certain amount of seller finance where the sales proceeds are paid over time by way of some form of earn-out or profit share.

Almost all management buy-outs, whether backed by a VC house or not, will require the management team to borrow against the existing assets of the business in order to raise the purchase price and will often also require the management team to borrow against their own assets (such as their property) in order to raise equity to put into the business. In order to help the management team raise as much money for the purchase and working capital going forwards as possible, the management team should contact an experienced asset finance brokerage in order to explore how best to raise money

against their personal and the business's assets (try
www.creativefinance.co.uk) and a checklist of the information
needed to arrange the debt funding of a management buyout is at
the end of this chapter.

Section 151 of the Companies Act prohibits a purchaser pledging the
assets of the company as security for money to be raised to buy the
company's shares. This provision is designed to prevent asset
stripping where a company with significant assets could in the past be
bought by someone with money raised from financial institutions on
the basis that as soon as they have bought the business, they will break
it up, sell off the assets and use the proceeds to repay the money they
have borrowed to buy the business. In practice the Act provides a
mechanism whereby so long as certain procedures are met, a
purchaser can borrow against the value of the assets being acquired in
order to fund a business purchase and professional advisors will be
required in order to prepare what is known as a 'whitewash
agreement'.

The Companies Act also imposes restrictions on the sale of
substantial business assets from the business to the directors (with
civil and criminal penalties designed to prevent directors looting the
company's assets without the knowledge of the shareholders). The
effect of this is that if a director wishes to purchase either substantial
assets (in effect anything with a value of over £100,000 or 10% of the
balance sheet) then under **Section 320** of the Companies Act, the
transaction requires the approval in advance of the shareholders.

In some businesses, such as say professional partnerships, it is often
the case that the partnership deed provides for dealing with the

retirement of partners at a specified age or set of circumstances on the basis of which their partnership share is acquired by other or new partners coming into the business.

If the intention is simply to hand the business over to junior family members coming up through the ranks, then no formal selling process may be required, although obtaining a formal valuation of the business and negotiating some form of structured buy-out of the retiring or older partner's interest so that authority is clearly handed over to the younger generation who are then free to manage the business as they see fit, is generally advisable. Situations where there has been no clear handover of power from one generation to the next (which are usually accompanied by the older generation retaining some form of paid interest in the business, as opposed to having had their share formally paid out), can lead to paralysis of the business as staff can be uncertain as to who is really in charge, and junior members of the family may be extremely reluctant to make any changes to the business for fear of doing something that may jeopardise the older member's income for which they may subsequently be blamed. A prolonged stalemate of this sort can do serious damage to businesses and in the long run can eventually lead to their failure.

If the business is not operated as a partnership, then there may be some form of shareholders' agreement specifying the basis on which an individual's shares may be sold to the other shareholders (usually on the basis of a formal valuation).

Looking outside the immediate employees and shareholders of the business, obvious potential purchasers of a business are its competitors within that industry or other businesses looking to enter the industry.

When considering how much they are likely to pay, other businesses within the industry may have an apparent advantage in that they may be able to increase the sustainable profit level by stripping out the central sales, accounting and administrative overheads where these functions duplicate services they already have. In effect, therefore, all they would need to bolt on to their existing business would be the increased level of turnover obtained from your customer base, plus the extra cost of sales in delivering that turnover and any overheads such as a sales force that are directly needed to carry on obtaining that business, enabling them to spread their administrative overhead over a greater volume of business. Against this, a purchaser coming in from outside will probably need to retain a greater level of overheads because your overheads are not duplicated in their existing structure.

Similarly, a purchaser from your trade will have better knowledge of the customer base, nature of product, risks and likely margins than someone coming in from outside. They should therefore have greater certainty over what it is they are actually buying and therefore need to discount less for risk than someone coming in from outside the industry.

This logic usually leads owner managers to conclude that a sale to someone within the industry is the most likely route to achieving a sale. It may therefore come as a bit of a surprise to learn that, in fact, purchasers from outside the industry may well be prepared to pay more than purchasers from within it.

This is because players within your own industry, once they know the business is for sale, will often conclude that the inherent disruption you will go through as part of the sale will give them the opportunity to get in and pick up some of your customers in any event by increasing their own sales effort without having to go to the expense of purchasing your entire business. They will therefore often be less inclined to rush out and purchase a business than many owner managers assume.

Additionally, businesses looking to buy their way in to a new industry are often prepared to pay a significant premium in order to do so. Once they have sold themselves on the idea that there is money to be made in this particular line of activities, it tends to be a motivation to get on with it (even if this means paying slightly more than may be necessary).

Players from outside the industry looking to get in will also be prepared to pay a premium to avoid the inefficiencies of starting a business from scratch and to be able to buy in specialist know-how and contacts that would otherwise take them a significant time to acquire. Again, potential purchasers within the trade will believe they already have this knowledge and contacts and will therefore not place a value on avoiding this 'learning curve'.

It is difficult to generalise but it is also the case that trade purchasers may well generally pay more than financial purchasers for any given business. Again this comes down to overheads, where a financial purchaser will need to retain the entire overhead structure of the existing business whilst a trade purchaser, even if not in a closely related business, will have some expectation of reducing some overheads by way of rationalisation of the two businesses and will generally also be expecting to gain some sales synergy from the cross-selling or the mutual benefits of merging the two organisations.

Finally, there is the sale of the business to the public, by way of a flotation where all the processes and documentation need to be undertaken in compliance with the relevant regulations. This activity requires a high degree of specialised professional advice and therefore lies beyond the scope of this book.

WHAT IF A BUYER COMES TO YOU?

Sometimes you do not have to reach prospective purchasers, they reach you with an unsolicited approach, either directly or through an advisor. Companies looking to expand through acquisition will commonly engage firms of corporate finance advisors to draw up a list of potential targets that fit their criteria and to approach these businesses to see whether they are for sale.

On the face of it this may seem quite an attractive option to an owner manager who is starting to consider a sale on the grounds that it will avoid much of the hassle of going through a sales process. Whilst this is true, you should consider:

◆ The advisor with whom you are dealing is looking after their client's interests (the buyer's) not yours as seller.

◆ If you commit to becoming involved in this sort of process without undertaking a full sale process, you are by definition only dealing with one purchaser, and therefore it is difficult to see how you can ensure that you achieve the best available price since you have not tested the value in the marketplace.

♦ There is also the danger that you are being bounced into a sale without proper professional advice on the purchaser's timetable and not yours, and without having taken the time to groom your business so as to achieve the best price in the negotiation. Against this must be set that you are dealing with a purchaser who is seriously interested in acquiring businesses in your sector.

♦ Bear in mind that the purchaser will be having similar discussions with other businesses in your sector and may therefore be able to run in effect a reverse Dutch auction where you and Joe down the road are competing to sell your businesses to the same party and may therefore be used to beat each other's price down.

Treat with caution therefore any such approach, and consider very carefully the pros of having a very interested and active buyer against the cons of your dealing on their terms not yours, before deciding whether to commit to the process.

HOW DO YOU REACH PROSPECTIVE PURCHASERS?

You may seek to obtain an offer by word of mouth, contacting people known to you, usually within your industry and enquiring whether they might be interested in buying the business. Whilst you may be able to directly contact some interested parties within your industry with a high level of credibility quite quickly using this method, it does have the dangers of limiting the pool of prospective interested parties to those you know, without exploring the potential of sales to financial institutions or to trade parties outside your industry, and if unsuccessful can leave you with the problem of being seen as tainted goods in the marketplace.

You can of course advertise your business for sale. You can place your advertisement in your own trade press, the national press, or some of the specialist business press. You can also advertise openly or covertly and directly yourself or through an agent.

The appropriate approach will depend broadly upon the nature and size of your business. If for example you are selling say a small sub-post office or shop, you might well consider advertising directly yourself through a publication such as *Dalton's Weekly*. You might also consider engaging an estate agent (preferably one that specialises in your field, eg Fleurets in the pub trade) to assist in selling the business who will act as both a broker to help negotiate the sale, but also as an advertising agent to ensure that the business for sale is publicised as part of the advertisements they run.

For a larger business you might consider advertising it for sale in say the national press (in which case you ought to use the business pages of the Sunday quality papers and the businesses for sale section of the *Financial Times* during the week). Most newspapers will offer a box number service that will enable you to maintain confidentiality of the name of the business for sale since all responses to the advert can be directed to a box number rather than the name of the business. This enables you to screen the replies received before deciding with which to proceed.

Additionally, there are now online listings of businesses for sale and business opportunities (such as www.equitymatch.co.uk and www.buyabiz.co.uk). You can use these in much the same way as you would use a *Financial Times* or other national press advertisement.

The limitation of the advertising approach is that it does not guarantee that the fact that your business is for sale is brought directly to the attention of people who may well be specifically interested in buying it.

The final method of reaching prospective purchasers and the one that I would recommend for any business of a reasonable size is to proactively identify potential interested parties and approach them with news that the business is for sale. This can of course be combined with a normal advertising approach in order to get the best of both worlds. As almost the first part of the selling process, your corporate finance advisor will generally discuss with you whether you have a list in mind of potential interested parties which will generally comprise suppliers, customers and competitors. Using this list as a basis, your advisor will then seek to expand it by searching databases to identify businesses of a relevant size and type within the same industry who operate in different areas who might wish to consider expanding in your locality, potential purchasers from outside your industry who might be interested in moving into it, and if your business has the right profile, potential financial purchasers who might be willing to back an MBI (a management buy-in to your business where a venture capitalist provides the funds for an external team of managers to buy your business in order to take it forwards). Your advisor will then prepare an initial approach letter, a sample format of which is set out below.

If you are concerned about the costs of engaging an estate agent or a corporate finance advisor to sell your business you might consider advertising it yourself in the appropriate media using a box number, and considering the responses you receive before deciding whether to engage a professional. So long as you can ensure that confidentiality is maintained, you have thereby not compromised your sales process and may indeed have generated a number of potential enquiries that your professional advisor can either follow up or use to suggest other prospective interested parties to approach.

Whichever method you choose, the important thing is to put together a structured plan as to how you are going to approach selling. After all to sell your particular products or services you will have had a marketing plan to target the appropriate prospective clients, have considered what it is they might want to know about your products in order to make them want to purchase, have approached them, provided them with the information, and looked to close the sale to get the deal done. The general principles of selling your business are going to be much the same.

Sample document – a typical initial approach letter

Here is an example of a typical approach letter by which your advisors will seek to generate interest in your business from potential purchases. An example of a confidentiality letter is given in Chapter 8.

Mr Prospect
Group Finance Director
Acquisition plc
London

Dear Mr Prospect

Acquisition Opportunity – Project XYZ

I am writing to you in the strictest confidence, to inform you that we are advisors to the shareholders of XYZ, a well-established, highly profitable widget company in the UK, who now wish to sell their investment in this business. We consider this to be an attractive opportunity which may be of interest to you.

Background

XYZ began trading in August 1995 as an incorporated business, however it has traded in various forms since the early 1970s.

The business is now the market leader in its field in importing and wholesaling widgets to UK retailers and distributors.

The unique position of the business enables it to achieve considerable margins unrivalled by its competition. As the company's reputation continues to grow the growth in turnover continues to be significant.

XYZ's rapid growth is set to continue as new markets have already been sourced.

The opportunity

The purchaser will acquire a business which has:

◆ an unrivalled reputation in its field
◆ the market leading position in widget imports
◆ a strong customer base
◆ experienced staff and management
◆ potential for expansion into other areas of the market
◆ significant growth potential
◆ well known branding.

Financial performance
Turnover for the year ended 31 July 2003 is forecast to be in the region of £51.1m with a pretax profit of £3.2m.

	1999 £(m)	2000 £(m)	2001 £(m)	2002 £(m)
Turnover	8.6	15.9	25.1	38.2
Adjusted profit before tax	1.0	1.3	1.8	2.4

Management and staffing
XYZ has an experienced management team, which operate the day to day running of the business, and employ 62 full-time staff.

Future prospects

XYZ has significant opportunities for growth in the future. Management forecast turnover to be around £80 million in 2004. There are new markets, such as the budget range of widgets (that have even greater margins than the high price widget range).

Further significant growth will come from the new products XYZ has developed complementing the original widget.

If you are interested in acquiring this business, please sign and return the enclosed confidentiality letter. I will then provide you with more detailed information on our client's business.

Please contact Mr Corporate Financier at your earliest convenience.

Yours sincerely

Corporate Financier

Text supplied by Horwath Corporate Finance

GOLDEN RULE 14

Be an active part of the sales process

Whilst your advisors may handle much of the practicalities of contacting prospective purchasers and getting them interested, they will be relying on you to make time to meet with prospective purchasers who are interested in buying your business, and the advisor's own staff who need to talk to the horse's mouth about all aspects of the business, and follow your advisor's advice about dealings with prospective purchasers.

WHAT ARE YOU GOING TO TELL PROSPECTIVE PURCHASERS?

You would not expect to sell your own products without a brochure or to achieve a sales appointment without having used some kind of mailshot, advertising, or sales promotion. Similarly you are going to have to actively market your business in a way that will stand out from the numerous proposals that any potentially active purchaser will be receiving.

You therefore need to make it as easy as possible for your potential buyers to decide they want to buy your business.

You do this by preparing a pack that sets out a description of the business and sufficient relevant information that can be read in no more than half an hour and that gives the reader all the necessary information to decide whether or not they wish to pursue this opportunity.

This sales pack (also known sometimes as an 'information memorandum', or technically, when issuing shares, as a **prospectus**) is such a crucial document it needs to be prepared and polished before contacting any interested parties.

It goes without saying that since this is the document on which interested parties will decide whether they wish to purchase the business, and also principally on which they will decide what price they are prepared to pay, it has to be accurate and true as the buyers will rely on it to make their offer. You therefore need to fully disclose all material facts as discovery of anything significant later on in the process, either before an offer is made or during due diligence, will hugely undermine the buyer's confidence in you and at worst will damage their trust in your honesty which may lead to a complete collapse in negotiations. The balance here is between presenting your company positively, and in a way that will attract the interests of buyers, while taking the opportunity to present the main weaknesses and risks of the business in their best light but from your point of view.

In addition, the sales pack needs to provide sufficient financial information to allow the buyer to properly assess the potential interest they have in the business. Given that their interest will be in sustainable profits going forwards, this obviously needs to reflect the work that your advisors will have done to establish the 'underlying' levels of sustainable profits, together with all relevant information the buyer needs to consider the overall financial situation. In addition to helping the buyer to screen whether your opportunity is of interest, giving all this information upfront will enable you to screen whether the buyer is really interested in your business. If you fail to provide sufficient information you may well find you are wasting time by providing the further information the buyer actually needs in order to decide that the deal is not for them.

CONTENTS OF A SALES PACK

The key aspects of any sales pack are detailed below.

Business background

- Summary of the current nature of the business and apparent opportunities.
- Summary of the current and projected operating results.
- Summary of the current balance sheet.
- Summary of the ownership structure.
- Summary of the reasons for sale.
- If seeking investment, how much investment is required, what it is to be used for, what return the investor can expect and in what timetable.
- Risks facing the business and steps taken to address them by management (say in the form of a strengths, weaknesses, opportunities and threats, or SWOT analysis).

Market

- Summary of products.
- Summary of markets and trends.
- Summary of customers.
- Summary of competitors.
- Summary of sale trends by product/market.
- Key competitive strengths.
- Assessment of competitors by product/market segment.
- Product/market segment growth and profitability.
- Branding.
- Sales staff.

Operations

- Product lines.
- Intellectual property.
- Suppliers and products.
- Management (including an organisation chart).
- Research and development.
- Opportunities identified (internally such as improved efficiency, and externally, such as new potential markets and products).

Assets

- Description of land and property.
- Description of plant and equipment.
- Description of data systems.

Appendices

- Current balance sheet, profit and loss account, forecasts.
- Product information and brochures.
- Summary CVs for key management.
- Employee details (giving number of employees, length of service, and age, which allows calculation of potential redundancy costs).

* List of trademarks and patents.
* Detailed lists of land and buildings, and major items of plant and equipment.

Any forecast or financial information provided should have any key assumptions made set out clearly and concisely. Financial information provided in the body of the report should be kept as simple as possible, with the detail available in the appendices. Any information in the appendices should tie up clearly and easily with information provided in the body of the report and be clearly cross-referenced.

The result must be a sales document that is easy to read and follow, giving a well structured account of the positive aspects of the business that does not drown the reader in detail.

GOLDEN RULES SUMMARY

14. Be an active part of the sales process.

Management buy-out financial information checklist

To raise money for a management buy-out by borrowing against the assets of the company you wish to purchase, use the following checklist to gather together all the information that an asset finance broker (such as Creative Finance www.creativefinance.co.uk) will require to arrange borrowings on your behalf.

Tick box when information collated

1 The deal

◆ Type of sale (share purchase or business and assets) ☐

◆ Purchase price ☐

◆ Expected working capital requirements following sale ☐

◆ Equity, grants, vendor financing (by way of deferred consideration or earn out) or other funding being put in (including details of MBO teams' investments in the deal) ☐

2 The business

◆ Industry and nature of trade ☐

◆ Trading history covering three years (with last audited and current management accounts) ☐

◆ The business forecasts (with underlying assumptions) ☐

◆ If in difficulty, details of the turnaround plan ☐

3 The management team

◆ CVs for all key team members ☐

◆ Personal wealth statements (house values less mortgages, other assets) ☐

4 The assets and liabilities

◆ Property: freehold or leasehold, valuation and description, details of any environmental/contamination issues, existing mortgages ☐

- ◆ Plant and machinery: valuation (or if not, asset listing with sufficient information re machinery make, model, age and condition to allow 'desktop' valuation), outstanding HP/lease liabilities ☐

- ◆ Debtors: aged debtors, aged creditors, sample invoice, contract and delivery note ☐

- ◆ Stock and confirmed orders: list of finished goods stock and confirmed order list ☐

8

The Pre-Sale Process

MANAGING THE SALES PROCESS

With your retained advisors generating enquiries and interest in buying the business, you will need to be involved in helping the sales process along.

In order to be prepared to deal with purchasers' initial enquiries, you should already have groomed the business, prepared much of the information they are likely to want to see and have to hand all the necessary basic documentation, to include:

◆ Detailed financial information, such as sets of accounts for the last three years and tax returns.

◆ Schedules of assets and liabilities, giving sufficient detail to enable the purchaser to form a clear view (for example, for leases and loans, indicate the balances outstanding, the interest rates applicable, and number and frequency of outstanding payments).

◆ Copies of all critical documents, such as leases, equipment leases, title documents, registered trademarks.

◆ Statutory books and records (which of course are up to date).

◆ Details of your external advisors.

As you go through this sales process be prepared to be sympathetic towards what may at times seem to be an inordinate number or duplication of requests for information, particularly when you reach the detailed phase of due diligence. It is important not to be surprised or irritated by the number of questions or the degree of detail covering everything from the important to the completely obscure and apparently irrelevant that you may be asked.

Bear in mind that you are looking for these people to pay a significant amount of money to you for your business. To obtain the maximum amount of money you want to leave them with the minimum number of outstanding queries or questions in their minds. It is therefore in your interest to ensure that every query, however apparently irrelevant or repeated, is politely and comprehensively dealt with. Comfort yourself with the thought that the more money they are likely to spend on buying your business, the more questions you might expect them to ask.

GOLDEN RULE 15

Understand that buyers want certainty

Much like buying a secondhand car, the thing that your buyer fears the most is that they are buying a 'pup' that you are getting rid of before some inevitable collapse or crisis comes home to roost. Your job is to be sympathetic to these concerns and do everything in your power to make them comfortable that they know sufficient about the long-term prospects and risks of the business to be able to invest in it.

Arrangements for initial meetings should be handled by your professional advisors with whom you should consult in advance of each meeting.

Your initial meeting with any interested party is your chance to make a first impression both in respect of yourself and your knowledge of the business and how you sell the business's prospects.

In order to prepare yourself for such meetings, you may want to have a member of your professional advisor's staff come in as a 'mock' interested party for a trial initial meeting and plant tour. Such rehearsals can prove invaluable in helping you formulate what you wish to say; how you wish to say it; and in which order to present the various aspects of your business. After all, the purpose of the initial meeting will be to ensure that the prospective purchasers go away impressed with the business, excited about the prospect of a sale, and keen for further face-to-face meetings in order to progress towards the sale.

Depending upon how you are dealing with the confidentiality issue, it may well be that the purchasers' opportunities to visit your business will be limited to this and possibly one other meeting before they are expected to make an offer, while they may obtain significant further information by way of papers deposited in a data room off-site (say at your advisor's premises) to which they are allowed access to review more detailed information away from the gaze of staff. In any event, your advisors should have had the prospective purchasers and their advisors sign a confidentiality agreement (see sample document below).

It therefore pays to be well prepared for these initial meetings and in advance of each meeting you should consult with your advisors. You obviously need to investigate who the potential purchaser is. If you understand why the potential purchaser is interested in acquiring your business, you are going to be better able to 'sell' those aspects of your business which fit in clearly with their strategy or business, for example that you have a stronghold in a particular area which fills a geographical hole in their coverage or a distribution network they can use. At the same time, your advisors should be investigating prospective purchasers to establish their likely ability to pay and track record in doing deals. If there is any likelihood that you will be expected to take some form of shares in the purchaser or any other form of deferred payment, you will obviously want to undertake research into the financial stability of the acquiring business and the prospects of actually realising your cash at some future point.

Attempt to establish in advance of the meeting, through your advisors, what particular areas of the business the prospective purchaser wishes to discuss or see and any immediate concerns they have so that these can be addressed.

As one of the purposes of this first meeting will be for the purchaser to indicate any areas of concern and raise queries they need answering, it is difficult to be too proscriptive about a formal agenda for the meeting, but in discussion with your advisors, you should set your own agenda covering the points you want to ensure you get across during the meeting in order to help the sales process. Demonstrate to prospective purchasers that you are serious about selling, evidently committing the time, both to preparing for the meeting and attending it. Ensure that you have cleared your diary in order to provide sufficient time for the meeting. Give instructions that you are not to be disturbed during the meeting, and if through discussion with your advisors you find that one of the things the purchasers want to see is the production department, or the sales staff, then ensure in advance that the production director, or the sales director, will be available on the day for the purchasers to meet and talk to.

In addition to being simple good manners and demonstrating commitment, ensuring that interruptions are avoided is also good tactics, as if the meeting were to be interrupted for something that only you could handle (particularly if it happens a number of times), it may give the purchasers the impression that you are indispensable to the business and weaken their confidence in the business's strength going forwards without you.

The overriding imperative must however be to remain open and honest about your communications and discussions with the purchaser. The objective of such meetings and discussions is to answer their enquiries so as to provide them with confidence in the business going forwards. Apparent reluctance to answer specific queries can lead to concerns that you are hiding something which damages confidence and therefore the price you will achieve.

It is about demonstrating your personal credibility as well as the business's credibility and therefore if you appear to be ignorant of significant facts relating to your business, it will damage your prospects of a sale. (This is one of the reasons why rehearsing with a mock initial meeting can be useful in helping to nail down areas where you need to do some revising so as to ensure you have all the facts and figures to hand.)

All businesses have their strengths and weaknesses, opportunities and threats, and face their risks. You need to balance being positive about promoting the opportunities and strengths of the business whilst being realistic about having identified the weaknesses and threats and being able to talk about the actions and contingency plans you have in place to overcome these to support the business going forwards.

In doing so you also need to achieve a balance between being seen to be obnoxiously eager, over confident and over proud about your business, its achievements and its potential, and the opposite of appearing to be apologetic or anxious about the list of downsides you feel the need to disclose to a prospective purchaser. Neither is helpful.

Once you have had your initial meeting with the purchaser, your advisor should be going back to them, after a suitably short period, to obtain some feedback as to their impressions and how they want to proceed.

If possible, you should ensure that you have some form of deputy, backup or representative who either your advisors or the prospective purchaser can reach if you are not available. Nothing causes more problems out of all proportion to the size of the original issue, than a buyer being unable to get a reply to simple questions as a result of you not being around or out of contact. Again, in order to impress upon the buyer that you are serious about selling, it may be worthwhile discussing during your initial meeting that all further questions should be passed to your representatives in their capacity as 'project managers' of the sales process. You can explain that you are obviously continuing to manage the business and to maintain the confidentiality of the sales process, but that you are keen to ensure all questions are dealt with as swiftly and as accurately as possible. Having all questions logged by your advisors so that they can track the process and ensure they have all been answered to the purchaser's satisfaction can reduce the risk of questions being overlooked or enquiries going astray at the company's premises.

Sample document – a typical confidentiality letter

Here is a typical confidentiality letter that you might expect your advisors (ABC Co Corporate Finance) to ask the purchasers (and their advisors) to sign as part of the initial sale process.

ABC Co Corporate Finance

Dear Sirs

Re: Project ('the Vendor')

This letter (the 'Confidentiality Letter') sets out the terms on which ABC Co Corporate Finance has agreed to make available to us certain confidential information relating to vendor companies ('the Vendor').

1 This letter covers all information both oral and written, communicated to us about the Vendor by or on behalf of the Vendor and by persons acting on behalf of any of the above. In the remainder of this letter such information is referred to as the 'Information'. The term 'Information' shall not include any Information which falls within any of the following categories:

(a) Information which has come within the public domain through no fault or action of ours; or

(b) Information which is in our possession, or one of our affiliates, at the time of disclosure by the Vendor or ABC Co Corporate Finance or which is independently discovered, after the date hereof, by us, or one of our affiliates, without the aid, application or use of the Information; or

(c) Information which is obtained, after the date hereof, by us or one of our affiliates, from any third party which is lawfully in possession of such Information and not in violation of any contractual or legal obligation to the Vendor or ABC Co Corporate Finance with respect to such Information.

2 The Information will be used by us only for the purpose of an evaluation of the Vendor in order to ascertain whether we should proceed with negotiations for the purchase of the Vendor.

3 The Information will be kept confidential by us and we will not disclose the Information or any part of it or extract from it to any person without ABC Co Corporate Finance's written consent.

4 We agree not to communicate with any person, other than those cleared, as notified in writing by ABC Co Corporate Finance about the existence of negotiations herefore and the progress hereof.

We further agree not to communicate with the management or any employee of the Vendor without prior written consent of ABC Co Corporate Finance.

5   We will not make any copies of the Information without ABC Co Corporate Finance's written consent. Such consent will only be given, if at all, for a specific number of copies to be taken, and numbered.

We further agree that only those members of our staff, who at our discretion need to have access to the Information in order to perform the evaluation of the Vendor, will be authorised to receive the same and then only to the extent needed.

6   We understand and acknowledge that while the Vendor believes the Information to be accurate, its disclosure to us is made without any express or implied warranty to that effect, and on behalf of itself and the other persons mentioned in paragraph 1, the Vendor and ABC Co Corporate Finance expressly disclaim any and all liability for representations, statements, or warranties contained in the Information or omissions.

7   We understand and acknowledge that ABC Co Corporate Finance may, at any time immediately by notice, require us to return the Information. In that event, or if prior to any such notice we have completed our evaluation and decided not to proceed with any further investigations into the Vendor, we will return or procure the return to ABC Co Corporate Finance of each and every copy of the Information which we have been given by ABC Co Corporate Finance or which has been made by us on our behalf, whether or not the same is then in our possession.

8   We understand and acknowledge the sensitive nature of the matter concerned and that we could become liable for any damages incurred by either ABC Co Corporate Finance or the Vendor in the event that we were to be found to be in breach of the terms set out herein.

9   The terms set out in this letter will be governed by and construed solely in accordance with English law and shall continue to apply for a period of two years, (unless in the meantime we have entered into a definitive agreement to purchase the Vendor).

The foregoing correctly sets out the terms which we hereby agree to observe as regards the Information disclosed to us.

Signed and accepted on the above terms.....................................

on behalf of..

Date ....

Text supplied by Horwath Corporate Finance

MANAGING THROUGH THE SALES PROCESS

While it varies greatly from one deal to another, the time it takes to sell a business will typically be longer than the owner initially expects for reasons that hopefully will become obvious as you read this book. During this period, you as the owner manager need to continue to manage the business both while the sale is proceeding, and as if no sale process was happening at all (as there is always the possibility that the sale may not conclude, in which case you do not want to have damaged your business by having started to run it without regard to its future).

Indeed, continuing to manage it on this basis is actually good practice in respect of the sale itself as running it with this approach is acting to support the long-term sustainable growth of the business which you are trying to sell.

It should also help you to continue delivering monthly figures throughout the sales process, vital for when the purchaser's accountants come in to do their due diligence, and look to see whether the trends of prior years are continuing during the current trading or starting to tail off, consideration of which will be vital to them in deciding whether your forecasts going forwards need to be qualified or revised downwards.

You also need to manage both the employees and knowledge about the sale. Broadly speaking, you should only be informing employees on a need to know basis, as until there is certainty as to the sale, advising employees that a sale is being contemplated is to cause them uncertainty about their future and the future of the business. This will be communicated in no short order to both your customers and your suppliers, each of whom will also become concerned about the prospects and future of the business, and also to your competitors who will take advantage of the situation.

The problems this causes are magnified if for any reason the sale then falls through, at which point staff will simply be wondering how long it is before they are up for sale again, competitors will be telling your customers the business obviously has a problem since the sale has fallen through and its future is uncertain, and suppliers will also be considering their situation.

Other than individuals who actually need to be brought into the loop, staff should only be informed about the deal once there is certainty, so that you can advise them who the acquirer is and you can also provide them with security as to the timetable for any changes and knowledge about what to expect.

In practice, if a sales process is conducted properly, employees need never really know until you need them to know. Sales packs should only be despatched to prospective purchasers once they have signed confidentiality agreements, a meeting and a tour of the plant can be arranged under a variety of pretexts (for example the prospective purchasers can pretend to be prospective customers who want to meet with the senior management and also tour the premises), key information that purchasers will need to review in detail can be provided through a data room arranged off-site, say at your advisor's premises, and if necessary follow-up meetings with prospective purchasers can also take place off-site at your advisor's premises.

GOLDEN RULES SUMMARY

15. Understand that buyers want certainty.

9

Negotiating the Price

THE NEGOTIATION PROCESS

Since the sale of your business is extremely complex and involves consideration of so many issues, you must expect negotiations to have significant ups and downs. Even if negotiations appear to break down altogether, it is best not to burn your bridges as you may be able to restart them at a later date. Your objective during the period leading up to the agreement of a sale price is to manage negotiations as positively as possible by paying attention both to the project management of the process and also by actively attempting to build consensus between yourself and the purchaser as to what has been agreed so that the remaining items for discussion can be gradually overcome.

The keys to successfully managing the negotiation process are as follows.

Listen to the purchaser

It is important to understand the purchaser's needs and wants and therefore their reasons for buying the business as well as the concerns that they need to address in order to feel comfortable in doing so. In particular, do not assume that the purchaser's concerns have gone away just because they have not mentioned them for some time. However, once you have agreed with them that a concern has been addressed, you should avoid unnecessarily reopening this as an area for them to consider.

Whilst listening, attempt to identify any particular issues in how the purchaser wants to structure the deal that may present you with a serious problem, given your objectives in the sale (for example you want to retire immediately, whilst the purchaser is evidently going to want to negotiate that you stay on for a number of years in order to smooth the transition).

The key to achieving this is to let the purchaser talk so that they can disclose their attitude towards the items under discussion. By contrast, some sellers become so focused on the need to 'sell' during negotiations that they appear to wish to dominate the conversation rather than negotiate an agreement between two parties. This leads on to the following.

Keep focused on your objective
Your objective is to reach an agreement to sell the business for an acceptable price and on acceptable terms so that you then keep the proceeds. It is not to dominate the conversation and you should try to avoid becoming emotionally involved (which is one reason for leaving much of the basic price negotiation to professionals working on your behalf). The buyer will be doing their job by making their opening offer a low price, at which point some sellers become insulted or upset and attempt to break off negotiation.

Remember that price negotiation is a process, not an immediate event, that will require you to interact with the purchaser in order to attempt to seek a deal which is acceptable to both sides. Retain a clear focus on your priorities and your target of a walkaway price, avoid becoming bogged down in unnecessary details (although appreciate that all the details will need to be covered by way of the final agreement), and remember it is a process with a purpose. What is important is achieving the sale and not in retrospect the process that led you there. Therefore remain flexible so as to be able to work round any objections or problems arising, and consider and make alternative proposals as part of the negotiation process. In a negotiation you should not expect to win every single battle and therefore it is important to prioritise your objectives so that you are in a position to trade concessions on items of lesser importance to you in order to obtain concessions from the purchaser on items of critical importance to you.

Be flexible

Whilst being flexible, remember that any business sale is not simply about the headline price for the business, but is also about the terms on which the deal is done. So be prepared to trade items to do with price against the nature of payment.

Be positive

Be positive and cooperative in your approach to the negotiations as at all times you are looking to increase the buyer's level of comfort and confidence in your business and in support of that, in you.

Be open and honest

Attempts to pull the wool over the purchaser's eyes will undermine their confidence and therefore the price they are prepared to pay. Always remember that any price you negotiate and agree at this stage will be subject to their detailed due diligence and the effect of uncovering adverse information (particularly if it appears this has been deliberately withheld during initial negotiations) will have a more significant adverse affect on the final price agreed and paid (and may even cause the deal to collapse altogether) than if information had been made available during initial discussions so it could be taken into account in negotiating the basic price.

Don't invent offers

Do not be tempted to create fictitious offers from non-existing alternative purchasers. If at this stage you are dealing with more than one prospective purchaser, it is appropriate to tell them and it is appropriate to put in place a sensible timetable during which to obtain offers from both interested parties. If you are in this position, you need to make clear to both parties how you are going to deal with considering such offers. You may consider getting each party to a position where you can conduct an auction (once one party has made an offer you go back to the second to see whether they will top it, before returning to the first to see whether they will increase their offer), which may seem a good way of increasing the offer price. However you will need to discuss this carefully with your professional advisors as unsurprisingly, many purchasers are unhappy at being placed in such a situation and the threat of such an auction may cause one or more to consider exiting the process.

If you attempt to use the prospect of a fictitious prospective purchaser to drive up the price of a real party you are negotiating with, you must expect that at some point the existence of this deception is likely to be discovered by the real purchaser, with potentially damaging consequences for the sale.

Don't walk unless you mean it

Whilst you must have your drop-dead price and must not therefore be afraid to walk away from any negotiation if it does not seem to offer the prospect of achieving this, you should only threaten to do so if you really mean it and if you have explored every other opportunity and option to try to negotiate around the problem. You should never grandstand on points of pride or ego in this process.

Leave doors open

If you reach the stage where you need to withdraw from discussions because it appears a deal cannot be reached, you should always attempt to end on a positive note, express your regret for the fact that you do not appear to be able to be in a position to conclude a deal with the purchaser at the present time, emphasise the points on which you have managed to reach agreement and leave a channel open for the purchaser to come back to you should they be willing to reopen negotiations over the points which at the moment cannot be resolved.

Know when to stop

Once you have achieved your objectives, stop. Bear in mind that just as you will have your drop-dead price below which you are not prepared to sell, the purchaser will have their walkaway price above which they are not prepared to pay. If you have achieved your objectives, do not be tempted to over-negotiate, as while you might obtain extra funds, you might drive away a perfectly acceptable deal.

GOLDEN RULE 16

Be flexible, patient, and proactive in negotiation

Putting together the perfect deal is difficult and achieving a successful sale will require both parties to be flexible and creative in negotiation. Once an offer has been received, study it carefully and come back with your constructive counter offers to help create a win-win situation for both sides and to keep the ball rolling.

STRUCTURING THE DEAL

Whilst much of the detail of structuring the deal will be negotiated during the period of due diligence and drawing up of the final sales contract, some of the overall elements will need to be thrashed out in order to agree the basic price and shape of the sale for incorporation into a formal offer letter from the purchaser to you that sets out the main terms of the proposed deal (known as heads of terms, or heads of agreement discussed in more detail later in this chapter).

Negotiations at this point are therefore not simply about price, but will also be about the overall shape of the deal.

Some of the principal issues that will need to be dealt with at this stage are detailed below.

How is the sale to be structured?

Broadly speaking if your business is operated through a limited liability company you will have two alternatives. Either as the owner of the shares in the company you can sell to the purchaser your shares, so that they have ownership of the legal entity that is the company, together with all its assets, business and liabilities; or the company can sell them its business and assets in return for cash or other consideration which then belongs to the company under your control.

For tax reasons (see Chapter 13), as a business owner, you are likely to want to sell the purchaser your shares. However for accounting reasons, the purchaser is more likely to want to buy the business and assets, as they then have choices as to how they account for those in bringing them into their own books which will affect the amount of goodwill they have to account for within their own accounts which they are also, as a result of recent changes in taxation, now able to write off against tax.

Additionally, if the purchaser buys the shares of the company, they are acquiring the company's liabilities as well as its assets. Whereas if they only buy the business and assets, other than some specific liabilities (such as the rights of employees which will be carried across and become rights against the new owner as the new employer under the Transfer of Undertakings, Protection of Employee Regulations, or **TUPE**), and any liabilities arising that relate directly to specific assets (such as the new owner takes over liability under the property or plant and equipment leases), the purchaser has limited their risk in the transaction as they will not be picking up any other liabilities the company may have.

If however the purchaser buys the shares, the company under their ownership continues to have all its own old liabilities. The worry for purchasers here is that there may be claims of which they are not aware that may subsequently arise and give them problems. For example, the company might have had some form of legal dispute which the owners quite reasonably feel can be defended or is unlikely to be pursued further by the other side. There is always the risk for the acquiring company, however, that the complainant may decide to take it further and may be successful. Alternatively the company may have supplied goods which have a warranty attached to them, and at the time of the sale there appears to be no problems with such goods in circulation, however at some point after the sale it transpires that problems have arisen that are covered by the warranty for which the company under its new ownership is now liable.

If a purchaser is to buy the shares of the business the seller must expect a more significant level of due diligence work to be undertaken in respect of potential liabilities so that the buyer can ensure they have avoided any of the above problems. Alternatively, if the buyer wishes to purchase only the business and assets, because of the adverse tax consequences for the seller, you may wish to seek a higher price from the purchaser to compensate you for the tax disadvantages of this method of sale.

How certain is payment going to be?

Many owner managers become so focused on the headline price of the sale, that they fail to take into account how this interacts with the terms of payment.

Leaving aside for a moment any payments made in respect of future profits above certain targets, consultancy after the sale, or interest on finance for the sale provided by the seller; the core of the deal will be a payment made by the purchaser to the seller for the business and assets or the shares in their company. This payment can either be made by way of cash or cash equivalent (within which I would include shares in the purchasing company where the shares are listed and readily tradable on a stock exchange, so that the seller can immediately convert some or all of the shares received into cash), or paper, by which I am referring to payment using instruments that are not immediately realisable by way of cash. Such paper instruments can include such things as:

- ◆ loan notes, whereby the purchasing company agrees to pay consideration over some period into the future

- ◆ options over the purchasing company's shares which are not immediately exercisable

- ◆ or shares where there is no immediate market through which you can turn them into cash (for example where the company is private and therefore not listed on any stock exchange).

Some deals will be a mixture of the two. As illustrated in the chart in Figure 6, the greater the element of cash or near cash in a deal, the greater your certainty of payment. The more paper there is in the deal, the less certainty you have of eventual cash outcome, and therefore you will seek a higher price to compensate you for this extra risk.

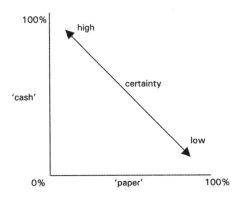

Figure 6. Composition of purchase price.

Case study
An Internet start-up sold a percentage of its equity to new investors (also in e-business) in return for listed shares in those investors valued at £8m. By the time the company decided to sell these shares in order to raise cash, the technology market had gone into decline and the shares were eventually sold for £4m.

How much are you financing?
Aligned to the above, what degree of the financing for the purchase are you going to have to provide? If you are in the fortunate position of selling your business to a cash rich purchaser, this may not be relevant. However in the case of many business sales, such as for

example, to a management team, the seller will end up financing part of the purchase price as the purchasers will not have enough cash available both to pay you for the purchase of the business, and to fund the working capital they will need going forwards to trade the business once they have bought it. If you are not prepared to provide some of the finance for the sale by way of giving them extended payment terms, you will in effect be reducing the amount of money they can afford to pay you for the business.

Payment to you for the business will come from money raised against the assets in the business, capital introduced by the purchasers, either from their existing cash reserves or by borrowing money against their personal assets, such as their houses, and finally, future trading. In order to maximise the amount of money available from the first two sources, it is important that the purchaser work with experienced asset finance brokers to raise the maximum amount of money that can be generated from both their personal and the corporate assets to be acquired. If the purchasers are not already in touch with such brokers, it can therefore be in your interests to ensure that they do so, try www.creativefinance.co.uk

Where you are helping to finance the sale by allowing the purchaser credit or agreeing to some form of payment over time by way of an earn-out, you do need to take precautions in order to reduce the risk you are taking.

If you do allow some deferred consideration, you should insist on having at least some of the consideration in cash so that the buyer has had to produce a significant down payment. You should ensure that the purchaser personally guarantees payment of the balance in addition to any contract signed by the purchaser's company. Where you are selling assets and are still owed money, you should take security by way of a charge over the assets sold so that in the event of the purchaser defaulting on payment, you can appoint a receiver to take over the assets and sell them on your behalf so you can be repaid. However you should appreciate that such security may be difficult to obtain and enforce.

Obtain credit references and credit searches on the purchaser, insist on being provided with regular sets of accounts, and ensure you have the right to inspect the company's books and records at any time.

Keep the period over which any extended period is to be paid to one that is reasonably short. However, equally importantly, allow a payment period to be sufficiently long to be practical. Having taken into account the likely sustainable profits to the business going forwards and the costs to the purchaser of servicing the rest of the debt they need to incur to buy the business from you, as well as funding working capital, ensure that the payments to be made to you leave enough in the business to provide both a cushion against any unexpected shocks and the purchaser with a decent living. Having the purchaser commit to such a high level of payments out of future income that the business either fails because it runs out of cash, or the purchaser decides to wind it up because they are not making any money out of it, are both self-defeating in the long term.

If you are providing finance for the deal by way of deferring payment terms, you should of course charge interest for the money you are effectively lending to the purchaser to buy your business. This is also high risk money as far as you are concerned (and you probably have no real wish to run a bank), and you also want to provide an incentive to the purchaser to find the money from other sources, be it finance companies, friends, or relatives. You should therefore charge a rate of interest that is significantly over the rates available for commercial loans at mainstream banks. If nothing else, this will also encourage the purchaser to pay off this money as soon as possible and therefore help to reduce your risk.

The best overall advice is generally to ensure that you obtain sufficient value up front in cash to meet your objectives and to treat deferred consideration as the icing on the cake!

GOLDEN RULE 17

Be prepared to finance

Insisting on an all-cash deal is likely to reduce the number of potential buyers and suggests that you may lack confidence in the future of the business. Financing the sale may mean you achieve a higher price, may help you in the timing of cash receipts for tax purposes and allow you to earn interest as a separate element of income but ensure you obtain enough initial cash.

How certain is the price?

The price you will achieve for your business will be largely determined by the confidence of the purchaser in the likely level of sustainable profits going forwards. Where there is any concern or dispute over the likely level of those profits, or the purchaser has difficulty in raising the full asking price by way of cash, use of an earn-out can be a way of bridging the gap between the price you are looking for and the upfront price the purchaser is either willing or able to pay.

An earn-out involves payment to you (in addition to the initial lump sum paid to you at the date of transfer) out of future trading profits.

The purchaser may also want to use an earn-out arrangement as a way of motivating you should you be staying on after a sale in order to help ensure the business achieves and beats the forecast profits.

The earn-out will usually be based on payment of either a specific percentage of profits or a percentage of profits over a specific target agreed between you and the purchaser.

An earn-out will usually last either one or two years. You may want to include within the contract a clause stating that in the event that the purchaser is able to sell on the business during this period for significantly more than they have paid you for it, you would also see a share of this profit (a **non-embarrassment clause**).

Be very careful about going into any earn-out arrangement however. Things will change in the business significantly over one or two years following a business sale and however tightly drafted, an earn-out agreement cannot realistically be expected to cater for all the changes of circumstance that may arise. There is therefore often significant potential for disputes arising between the buyer and seller over how the earn-out is worked and you should only therefore go into it if you are very confident of your ability to manage the ongoing relationship with the purchaser following the sale.

Any arrangements for an earn-out need also to cover a number of specific points so as to minimise areas of dispute. If you are going to be rewarded out of future profits, then you will need to agree with the purchaser how certain items are going to be managed so as to ensure that profits do not meet expectations for reasons outside your control. These include the impact of any accounting policies that the purchaser wishes to use that differ from the existing ones upon which the forecasts have been based; any cross-charges that the purchaser is intending to make to the business (for example by way of group 'management charges'); how any financing costs that are either cross-charged from elsewhere in the group or have been incurred by the purchaser to buy the business impact upon your forecasts of achievable profits; and commitments that the purchaser will make in investments (for example in plant and machinery, or maintaining or increasing advertising expenditure), upon which the forecast profits and targets have been based.

Obviously, if you are going to be rewarded by the profits generated from the business over a specific period, you are going to want to maintain control of the business during that period and so you may well need to have written in to the contract that you will be retained as managing director throughout the period of the earn-out.

If you are considering some form of earn-out based on your forecasts as to how the business is likely to perform following the sale, if possible undertake some research into businesses previously acquired by the purchaser to see how well they have managed previous acquisitions. One thing you must expect as the result of any sale is that how your business is operated will change. The purchaser will have different ideas about how things are to be done and to be managed and if it is an established group, will have its own operating rules and procedures. Insofar as you are able to do so, the more you can find out about how acquisition by this purchaser has impacted on prior businesses they have bought, the better you can judge the likely impact of the sale on the prospects for your business and therefore on your earn-out.

How much support is the buyer going to need after completion of the sale?

Will the buyer need you to stay on for a month or two to allow you to train them in running your business? May they need you to stay on for one or two years in order to ensure a smooth handover of contacts, relationships and clients?

What restrictions will the purchaser place on you as part of the sale?

Almost every sales contract is likely to include some form of non-competition covenant whereby you undertake not to set up a new business in competition with the one you have just sold within a specified time or area. Obviously your own circumstances and objectives in achieving the sale will have a significant impact on how strong or far reaching a covenant you are going to be able to live with. If, for example, you are simply looking to retire, then the effect of such a covenant may be completely irrelevant to you. If however you are looking to cease trading your own particular business but may be interested in doing say, consultancy in this area in the future, then you are going to need to think very carefully about what wordings for such a covenant will be acceptable to you.

GOLDEN RULE 18

Terms are as important as price

Since the negotiation of price is not simply about price, but also about broad terms of the deal, in addition to your target and drop-dead price you must have given thought to the objectives you are trying to achieve and your views as to your preferred deal terms including the incentives you are prepared to give before getting into these negotiations.

HEADS OF TERMS

By the end of this process you should reach the point where you have agreed the basic price and terms of the sale with the buyer, and you will be in position to agree heads of terms or heads of agreement.

This usually takes the form of a formal letter from the purchaser to you confirming the general outline of the purchaser's offer which you have agreed to accept, subject to contract.

As such you will expect the heads of terms to set out broadly:

◆ The price, either by way of a specific number (£Xm), or by way of some kind of formula (X% of profit over the next three years paid annually three months after the end of the year).

◆ The deal structure, either a sale of shares or a sale of business and assets (in which case if there are any assets which are to be specifically excluded, for example land or property or debtors, these should be noted).

◆ Specific description of the purchaser's requirements from you, such as your staying on for a specified period as an employee or under a consultancy agreement, and details of the proposed non-competition covenant.

◆ Conditions attached to the offer such as the need for audit and due diligence (in which case there needs to be some indication as to the scope of work required and how the process is to be managed, particularly in respect of access to staff, papers and maintenance of confidentiality).

◆ Exclusivity. Having reached this point the purchaser can now expect to start to incur significant professional costs as they will need to instruct their professional advisors to undertake formal due diligence and the detailed negotiations of the sales contract. Since the purchaser knows that they are going to have to spend money on this activity, not unreasonably most purchasers want to ensure that they are not wasting their time doing so and will therefore demand that you agree for a limited period of time to deal exclusively with them in order to give them a fair chance of completing the transaction.

Whilst unless there are particular circumstances it is not unusual to agree to such a condition, it is important to ensure that this period is limited to a specific period sufficient to allow due diligence to take place and a contract to be agreed (say 45 to 90 days), otherwise you are simply giving the prospective purchaser an exclusive option over your business from now until such time as they might decide to exercise it or not. In addition, by placing a time limit you focus their minds on the need to complete the deal before other parties can become involved again.

♦ The offer may also give specific conditions that have to be met in order for the deal to proceed (such as the net worth remaining over a specified sum or regulatory approval, or the purchaser's raising funds) or set out events that will cause the deal to fail (such as the loss of specified key customers or issues in respect of financial assistance).

It is important to stress that the heads of terms is essentially a **letter of intent** to complete a deal and is not the contract for sale itself. It is important however, for a number of reasons, as:

♦ It marks the stage at which you have an offer that you have negotiated and agreed with the purchaser.

- ◆ It does have legal implications (and therefore you should take legal advice about accepting it) in that, for example, you are comfortable with the terms under which you are agreeing to any period or form of exclusivity to the purchaser.

- ◆ It provides a degree of moral commitment on the part of the purchaser to move towards completing a deal.

- ◆ The granted period of exclusivity clears the decks for the purchaser to commit to what is for them the most expensive part of the process leading up to a sale.

- ◆ It provides written evidence of the structure of the deal and terms you have agreed with the purchaser.

However it is important to realise that the purchaser has made this offer before carrying out detailed due diligence. It is therefore an offer made based on the information you have provided (on which the purchaser is relying at this stage). Once the purchaser's advisors gain access to your books and records to conduct their proper due diligence, if significant issues arise they will obviously have a serious impact on the price that is finally agreed for the sale.

SAMPLE DOCUMENT – A TYPICAL HEADS OF TERMS AGREEMENT

The following is an example of the format that heads of terms will take showing how, subject to contract, due diligence, maintaining or achieving certain specified performance benchmarks and negotiation of the detailed terms, the basic outline of the sale agreement is summarised and the purchaser is given access and a period of exclusivity within which to seek to close the sale.

Mr Seller ('Vendor')

XYZ Ltd ('XYZ')

and

Mr Buyer ('Purchaser')

Heads of Terms: Subject to Contract

Mr Buyer will purchase the entire issued share capital of XYZ, free of all encumbrances and charges.

The Consideration

The total consideration for the purchase of XYZ shall be £15.2 million to be satisfied as follows:

a) Payment of £10.2 million in cash on completion.

b) Payment of £2 million in loan notes to be issued at completion payable if the operating profit for the year ending 30 November 2004 exceeds £3 million. Payment to be made on agreement of the audited results for year ending 30 November 2005.

c) Payment in loan notes at completion of a maximum of £5 million on the basis of £10 for every £1 that the aggregate operating profits exceed £5.2 million for the two years ending 30 November 2005. Payment to be made on agreement of the audited results for the year ending 30 November 2005.

For the purposes of calculating the operating profit for the years ending 30 November 2004 and 2005 an external management charge will be made against these profits of £9,000 per month from the date of completion. This will be a fixed charge regardless of the actual cost of the management. For the avoidance of doubt, this management charge does not include any current management of XYZ.

The payment in c) above will be reduced by the actual payment made in b) above.

Conditions Precedent

Completion of satisfactory due diligence for this type of transaction.

Mr Seller entering into a consultancy agreement for two years from completion for 25 hours per week.

The business achieving adjusted operating profits for the year ending 30 November 2003 of £2.6 million.

The group being debt free with net assets of at least £1.1 million at 30 November 200X, subject to sufficient working capital at completion.

Earn-out

The agreement will contain reasonable earn-out protections appropriate for a transaction of this nature.

Warranties and Indemnities

The Vendor will give reasonable warranties and indemnities in relation to XYZ appropriate to an arm's length transaction of this type, with usual limitations on liability.

Pensions

The Vendor confirms that XYZ does not operate any pension scheme for its officers or employees.

Property

Prior to completion the property assets in the balance sheet of XYZ will be transferred to the Vendor with no adverse cash or taxation consequences. The owner of the property will grant to the company a lease on commercial terms at prevailing market rent.

Access and Due Diligence

The Purchaser will have access to the records, documents and papers of XYZ sufficient to carry out their due diligence requirements.

The Purchaser will have reasonable access to the senior management of XYZ during the due diligence period.

Non-competition

Mr Seller (for himself and on behalf of his related parties, being any person connected to him within the meaning of S.345 of The Companies Act 1985) will enter into appropriate arrangements in respect of non-competition in relation to the current business and its employees, suppliers and customers in a mutually acceptable form. The period of restriction will be for a period of sufficient duration to protect the goodwill of XYZ.

Exclusivity

In consideration of the Purchaser incurring costs of professional advisors and other expenses and expending further management time in considering the proposal to acquire XYZ the Vendor agrees with the Purchaser that during the period from the date of acceptance by the Vendor of the terms of this letter until the earlier of 1 August 200X, completion of the Acquisition or the date on which discussions regarding the Acquisition are terminated by mutual agreement, the Vendor will not make any initial or further approach to or enter into or continue any discussions with any third party with a view to disposal of XYZ or any part thereof to any person other than the Purchaser.

Confidentiality

The matters contemplated by this letter are to be treated in strictest confidence and should not be disclosed to any person whatsoever without the prior written consent of the other party hereto. In the event that the Acquisition is not completed, the Purchaser undertakes that it will not disclose or make use of, for its own benefit, any of the information of a confidential nature relating to XYZ, which has been disclosed to the Purchaser. The provisions of this paragraph do not apply to any information, which is publicly available at the time of disclosure unless disclosed through breach of this undertaking, nor does it apply to any information disclosed by the parties to the extent that disclosure is required by law or regulation.

Costs

The Vendor and the Purchaser agree to bear their own legal, accountancy and other costs and expenses incurred in connection with the negotiation, preparation and implementation of this letter and the Acquisition. The Purchaser undertakes to prepare the first draft of the sale and purchase agreement in connection with the Acquisition.

Governing Laws and Jurisdiction

This letter (and any dispute, controversy, proceedings or claim of whatever nature arising out of or in any way relating to this letter or its formation) shall be governed by and construed in accordance with English law.

Each of the parties to this letter irrevocably agrees that the courts of England shall have exclusive jurisdiction to hear and decide any suit, action or proceedings, and/or settle any disputes, which may arise out of or in connection with this letter (respectively, 'Proceedings' and 'Disputes') and, for these purposes, each party irrevocably submits to the jurisdiction of the courts of England.

Timing

It is intended that the transaction will be completed by 1 July 200X.

Signed by:
Mr Buyer for and on behalf of the Purchaser ....

Mr Seller the Vendor ....

GOLDEN RULES SUMMARY

16. Be flexible, patient and proactive in negotiation.

17. Be prepared to finance.

18. Terms are as important as price.

10

Due Diligence

WHAT IS DUE DILIGENCE?

Due diligence is the term used to describe the detailed investigation and audit undertaken by the purchaser prior to exchanging contracts. It is akin to the way in which once you have seen a house advertised and you make an offer to buy it, before exchanging sales contracts you have a survey carried out to ensure there is nothing untoward that might affect your decision to complete the purchase.

In moving towards closing a sale, having achieved heads of terms, due diligence and the negotiation of the detailed sales contract will tend to run in parallel as the treatment of issues arising out of the due diligence process will need to be negotiated for inclusion in the contract.

Traditional due diligence has always focused on legal and financial matters. Over the last few years however a broader 'commercial' due diligence has increased in importance.

There is significant crossover between these three broad areas as shown in Figure 7.

The areas to be considered under each of these broad headings are set out below and are all areas that should be addressed during your grooming of the business for sale so that due diligence goes as smoothly as possible.

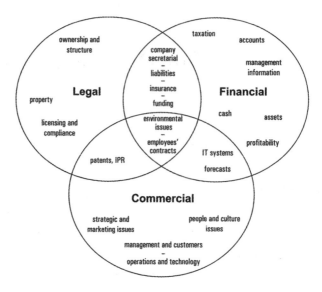

Figure 7. Interlocking fields of due diligence.

LEGAL DUE DILIGENCE

Legal due diligence is broadly about establishing the basic
information surrounding the company and the legal status of its
relationships with other parties so that problems can be spotted and
adequate warranties taken; ensuring the company's compliance with
the regulatory framework within which it needs to operate; as well as
establishing the legal position in respect of a number of specific
areas of assets and liabilities which may affect the final structure of
the deal.

The main areas to be covered are set out below.

Ownership and structure

As the solicitors will need to prepare a sales contract, first and
foremost they will be interested in who are the parties to the
contract. Legal due diligence will reveal the business's formal legal

structure – a partnership with a partnership deed, or a company with authorised share capital. If it is a company they will need to know what is the authorised issued share capital, who are the shareholders, are there any agreements between shareholders, are there any restrictions on the shareholders' ability to sell shares, or restrictions in the company's memorandum and articles of association that will impact on the ability to do the proposed deal.

The solicitors will also want to know whether any of the shares, or the company's assets, have been offered as security to any third party (for example, a debenture given to secure loans from a bank).

There will be checks to ascertain whether the business is solvent and whether there are any insolvency or other legal proceedings pending and if so, the detailed status of each item.

They will also need to ensure that there are no other bars to completing a sale, such as: do any contracts, licences or agreements entered into by the company require the consent of any third party to the sale and change of ownership of the business?

Statutory compliance

The solicitors will need to check that the statutory books and records are up to date, reflecting all the currently issued shares, meetings of directors, debentures and other charges, and whether the business has filed all necessary tax and/or company secretarial returns (such as filing of annual returns and sets of accounts at Companies House).

Funding facilities and liabilities

Any or all loan and related security or guarantee documentation will need to be reviewed.

Are the business's banking facilities in place with up to date mandates? Have the directors and/or owners personally guaranteed any such facilities? If so, how is it proposed that such facilities will be dealt with?

Details of any grants received will be reviewed to see whether the potential sale may make these liable to be repaid.

Has the business given any guarantees or indemnities in respect of any third party's obligations and do any third parties have any options over the company's shares or any of its assets?

A complete list of all disputes, claims, and any known legal proceedings will be required, together with full details of progress of the case and the company's position.

A full list of all contingent liabilities, including employee claims, guarantees, warranties, product returns, maintenance and support obligations, and any claims from suppliers for payment that are being disputed will be needed.

Contractual relationships

The team will want to review all material agreements with suppliers or customers, such as any joint ventures or partnerships, any agencies, licences, distribution agreements, franchising, or outsourcing arrangements, and any material supply contracts with customers or suppliers. They will also need to review any standard contracts for sale of goods or supply of services as well as standard purchasing documentation.

Reservation of title clauses built into your terms of sale and the details and potential exposure under all warranties that you offer with your goods and services will need to be reviewed.

The list of material contacts will be reviewed to establish whether any of the business's contracts are directly with either the individual vendors or related parties, and if so, whether any of these are undertaken on the basis of arms length transactions or on non-commercial terms.

Licensing and compliance
The solicitors will need to check that you meet all the necessary regulations and licensing requirements for carrying out your trade, and whether you are in default of any regulatory matters.

Where appropriate a detailed health and safety review will be undertaken (which may involve the employment of a specialist) and will require full disclosure of all health and safety meetings, recent reviews and inspections, and any disputes.

Similarly, a view will need to be taken by the purchaser as to the extent to which an environmental due diligence is required, although given the strictness of current environmental legislation, this is almost becoming inevitable in a business sale of any size. Again a specialist reviewer may well be involved to consider the potential environmental risks of the company's business, review the necessary licensing and consents and to review compliance with rules and regulations concerning waste discharges, spillages and so on.

There will also be checks to ensure the company is properly registered under the Data Protection Act and is complying with the requirements of the Act.

Intellectual property

A key part of the business's value is its ownership of licences or **intellectual property (IPR)**, such as trademarks, brand names, patents or designs. These will be checked to ensure that all such intellectual property has been registered where applicable with the relevant authorities, such as the trademark registry or the patent office and that this has been done in the company's name (and not the name of the owner).

Is there any intellectual property of significant value which has not been registered? Does the company trade under its own corporate name or under other trading names? If so have these been properly protected by registering as trademarks and possibly by registering dormant limited liability companies under these names at Companies House? If so, who owns these dormant companies, the business owner or the company? Has the company registered domain names so as to protect its trading names in e-commerce? Is the business party to any confidentiality agreements?

Employees

Employees can be a major source of claims against a company. The team will require a detailed list of all current employees, together with copies of your standard terms and conditions of employment.

Do any employees have materially different terms and conditions of employment? If so, you will need to provide copies. What are your procedures for dealing with procedures, complaints and disciplinary matters? You will need to provide details and your records of such activities. Provide details of all employees who have been dismissed over the last say three years. Are there any cases pending for unfair or constructive dismissal?

Have any employees been dismissed within the last six months? Are there any cases currently at an employment tribunal? Has the company engaged the services of a professional firm of employment advisors in order to ensure its procedures and practices match the requirements of current employment law?

Are there are any profit sharing, bonus or option schemes for directors or employees? If so, provide details.

What pension arrangements are offered by the company to employees? If there are more than five employees, has the company instituted, at minimum, a stakeholder pension scheme? The company will need to provide details of all existing pension schemes and, if the company operates any form of final salary scheme, you will need to provide details of actuarial valuation so that the degree of funding can be established, as well as details of the employer's obligations and names of the trustees.

They will need to review copies of all contracts of employment for directors (often known as service agreements). In addition to basic information about salary and notice periods, do such contracts include provisions for restrictive covenants preventing them from entering into competition with the company, specific bonus, profit sharing or option schemes and/or provisions specifically regarding the sale of the business (for example, a 'golden parachute')?

Property

The solicitor will need a list giving the details (address, whether freehold or leasehold, and if leasehold length of the lease and name of the landlord) of all properties used by the business, together with all the documentation needed to be able to establish that you have good title of these properties in order to be able to hand them over to the purchaser.

The solicitors will need to investigate a range of commercial issues around all such properties including the terms of leases, details of any specific rights or restrictions on your rights to deal with the property arising out of any transactions such as mortgages, charges, easements, subtenancies, or options that have been granted, either to or from the business. Often a surveyor's report will be requested to provide a valuation of the property together with a costing of any dilapidations that may exist and for which the business is liable under the lease.

Key issues will include:

◆ Are there any disputes with the landlord or owners of adjoining premises?

◆ What planning exists in respect of the properties, and have all the necessary planning permissions and building regulations necessary for the business's required use been obtained?

◆ Is there any planning consent for use other than as currently that might have an affect on the property's value?

◆ Who is responsible for insuring the property, the business or the landlord? If it is the company, provide details of the insurance.

- Does any change of ownership of the company require the landlord's consent?

- How long do any leases have left to run?

- What are the current rentals and when, and on what basis, are rent reviews conducted?

- Has the company previously rented property where it has then signed the lease to a third party? If so, does the company still have a **contingent liability** in respect of that lease?

- Are there any specific environmental risks associated with any of the properties such as a history of contamination or subsidence?

Insurance

Does the business have adequate insurance to cover its assets, as well as its trading activities (such as business interruption cover, and product liability insurance)? Provide copies of all the insurance documentation together with details of any outstanding claims in progress.

Sample document – legal due diligence questionnaire

If all this seems demanding, set out below is a sample legal due diligence questionnaire suppliled by Ward Hadaway.

Legal Due Diligence Questionnaire (Target)

Contents

1. Introduction
2. Constitution of the Company
3. Accounts
4. Litigation

5.   Plant and equipment

6.   Business of the company

7.   Intellectual property

8.   Information technology

9.   Directors

10. Employees, consultants and sub-contractors

11. Pensions

12. Taxation

13. Properties

14. Environmental

1. Introduction

TO: **The Directors of [Target]**

FROM: **Ward Hadaway**

1.1.   References in this questionnaire to the 'Company' are references to [target] and all of its subsidiary companies (if any). Please therefore reply to each enquiry for [target] and all its subsidiary companies (if any).

1.2.   Please supply a copy of the documentation and/or supply the information requested in this questionnaire in relation to the Company and identify replies by using the same numerical reference system. In the event that there is no documentation or information in relation to a particular company, please confirm there is none in the reply to that enquiry.

1.3.   In the case of any copy documentation, please ensure that each copy is complete and where a full understanding of the position cannot be obtained from the copy document(s) alone please also provide an explanation. Where details have been requested, please reply as fully as possible to avoid any further enquiries.

1.4.   We suggest that you supply responses as and when the information is available rather than waiting until all the information has been collected.

1.5.   [The replies to this questionnaire (and any further enquiries raised by Ward Hadaway) will form the basis of a formal legal due diligence report about the Company to be prepared by Ward Hadaway and issued to [   ] as instructed by you.]

1.6.   This questionnaire is not exhaustive and supplemental requests for information and/or documentation may be made by the appropriate department of Ward Hadaway.

1.7.   Please address all responses to and queries about this questionnaire to [   ] on [   ]; e-mail:] or [   ] on [   ]; e-mail: [   ]

2. Constitution of the Company

2.1.   Please provide a copy of the current Memorandum and Articles of Association of the Company and any amending resolutions in relation to the same.

2.2.   Please provide the names and company registration numbers of the Company and all companies in which the Company holds, or has agreed to hold or to acquire, shares and, in the case of each such company, specify:

2.2.1.   the authorised and issued share capital;

2.2.2.   the names of the shareholders and the number and class of shares held by them;

2.2.3.   the product manufactured and/or the service supplied; and

2.2.4.   the general nature and scale of operations.

2.3.   Please supply copies of all agreements relating to the ownership and/or control of the Company.

2.4.   Please supply copies of all options and agreements relating to the issue or transfer of shares in the Company.

2.5.   Please deliver the statutory books (and any separate minute book(s)) of the Company to Ward Hadaway. The statutory books will be returned following inspection.

2.6.   Please supply copies of all declarations of trust and other deeds and documents governing the trusts upon which any shares in the Company are held, together with the names and addresses of all trustees.

3. Accounts

3.1.   Please supply copies of the audited accounts of the Company for each of the last three years.

3.2.   Please supply details of any changes in accounting policy over the last three sets of audited accounts.

3.3. Please supply copies of all unaudited draft accounts of the Company.

3.4. Please supply copies of the most recent Management Accounts of the Company.

3.5. Please supply copies of the current year's budgets.

3.6. Please supply copies of all current Business Plans.

3.7. Please provide a schedule itemising:

   3.7.1. current debtors, period of debt and amount; and

   3.7.2. current creditors, period of credit and amount.

4. Litigation

4.1. Please supply details of all prosecutions, proceedings, litigation, arbitration, mediation or other forms of dispute resolution in which the Company is or is likely to be engaged, or has been engaged in the previous three years.

4.2. Please supply details of all outstanding complaints or disputes (including any intimated by or intimated against) the Company in relation to:

   4.2.1. any materials or goods (or class of materials or goods) supplied by the Company; and/or

   4.2.2. any services (or class of services) rendered by the Company; and/or

   4.2.3. any other aspect of the business of the Company.

4.3. Please supply details of any subsisting circumstances or grounds which are likely to give rise to:

   4.3.1. any prosecutions, proceedings, litigation or arbitration involving or concerning the Company; and/or

   4.3.2. any complaint or dispute (as referred to at 4.2 above).

4.4. Please supply details of all accidents at work which have or could have given rise to a claim against the Company (whether or not covered by insurance).

4.5. Please supply details of all material breaches that have occurred under any contracts or arrangements to which the Company is a party.

4.6. Please supply a copy of the Company's accident record book.

4.7. Please supply a copy of the health and Safety at Work Act etc. procedures.

5. Plant and equipment

5.1.   Please supply a copy of all up to date plant and machinery registers giving details of the location of this plant and machinery.

5.2.   Please supply details of all plant and equipment (excluding computer equipment) used by the company subject to leasing, credit sale, hire purchase or similar arrangements.

5.3.   Please supply details of any equipment used by the Company but owned by another member of the Company's group or any third party and details of the arrangement in respect of the use of such plant and equipment.

6. Business of the Company

Finance

6.1.   Please supply details of all banking and financial arrangements operated by, or available to, the Company, and please also supply copies of all agreements, facility letters and/or other documents relating to the same.

6.2.   Please supply copies of the following:

6.2.1.   all legal charges, debentures, mortgages or other financial or security documents affecting the Company, or other documentation relating to the same; and

6.2.2.   all loan agreements affecting the Company or other documentation relating to the same.

6.3.   Please supply copies of all hire purchase, leasing, credit sale, or deferred payment agreements or similar arrangements to which the Company is party.

6.4.   Please supply details of any guarantees, sureties or indemnities (or assurances of a similar nature) which have been given by or for the benefit of the Company.

Insurance

6.5.   Please supply details of all policies of insurance maintained by the Company, and a copy of the policy documents and any other agreements and/or documents relating to the same (including any insurances relating to life assurance, permanent health insurance and medical expenses insurance).

6.6.   Please supply details of all insurance claims made by and against the Company — both current claims and those made by and against the

Company within the last three years.

6.7. Please confirm that the Company has paid all premia on its insurance policies.

6.8. Please supply details of credit insurance effected and claims experience.

Grants

6.9. Please supply details of all investment, employment, local authority or central government grants which have been paid or awarded to the Company (including the terms and conditions of repayment) and please also supply a copy of all agreements and other documentation relating to the same.

Trading

6.10. Please supply copies of the following:

6.10.1. all agreements and written contracts terminable upon the transfer of shares in the Company;

6.10.2. any outstanding quotations or tenders made by or to the Company;

6.10.3. all standard terms and conditions of trading issued by the Company. Please also supply details of when and how such terms and conditions are used;

6.10.4. all standard terms and conditions of trading issued by third parties which affect the Company. Please also supply details of when and how such terms and conditions are used.

6.11. Please supply copies of all agreements and/or other documentation relating to the following:

6.11.1. all licences or consents granted by, or in favour of, the Company;

6.11.2. all registrations held by the Company that are necessary or desirable to conduct its business;

6.11.3. all material or long term agreements or arrangements to which the Company is a party;

6.11.4. all maintenance agreements or arrangements to which the Company is a party;

6.11.5. all agency agreements or arrangements to which the Company is a party;

6.11.6. all distribution agreements or arrangements to which the

Company is a party; and

6.11.7. all factoring agreements or arrangements to which the Company is a party.

In the case of any such licences, consents, registrations, agreements or arrangements (referred to in 6.11.1-6.11.7) not reduced to writing, please supply a summary of their terms, including the names of the parties, commencement date, termination date, duration and termination provisions.

6.12. Please supply details of all arrangements between the Company and the Company's competitors (whether legally enforceable or not) and supply a copy of all agreements and other documentation relating to the same.

6.13. Please supply details of the trade associations of which the Company is a member, if any, including copies of any rules or code of conduct of such association(s) or agreements between members with which the Company should comply.

6.14. Please supply details of all agreements, arrangements or transactions to which the Company is or has been a party for the transfer of any assets at undervalue within the period of 2 years preceding the date of this questionnaire.

6.15. Please supply a list of major customers of the Company (ie those accounting for more than 5% of its turnover) and the value of sales to each in the last 3 years.

6.16. Please supply a list of major suppliers of the Company (ie those accounting for more than 5% of goods or materials purchased) and the value of purchases from each in the last 3 years.

6.17. Please provide details of any restrictions on the Business to conduct its business and copies of all agreements and/or other documents relating to the same.

6.18. Please supply details of any supplier or customer where the relationship is likely to change because of the sale of the Company or for other reasons (including full details of the last 12 months' purchases or sales and orders in hand).

6.19. Please supply details of any significant capital or reserve commitments.

7. Intellectual property

7.1. Please supply details of:

7.1.1.   all patents or applications for patents vested in, or used by, the Company;

7.1.2.   all registered and unregistered trade marks, trade names and brand names vested in, or used by, the Company;

7.1.3.   all registered and unregistered service marks vested in, or used by, the Company;

7.1.4.   all registered designs vested in, or used by, the Company;

7.1.5.   all design rights vested in, or used by, the Company;

7.1.6.   any material in which the Company has, or claims, a copyright interest or database right;

7.1.7.   all other intellectual property rights vested in, or used by, the Company;

7.1.8.   all domain names owned or used by the Company.

In each case provide the date of application, date of grant, and registration number, and details of actual use over the last three years anywhere in the world, as appropriate.

7.2.   Please supply copies of the following:

7.2.1.   all agreements, licences or arrangements to which the Company is a party affecting or relating to the development of any intellectual property rights vested in, or used by, the Company or where such agreements, licences or arrangements are not in writing, please supply a summary of their terms, including the names of the parties, commencement date, termination date, duration and termination provisions.

7.3.   Please supply details of any of the rights referred to above which are shared with any other members of the Company's group of companies.

7.4.   Please supply details of any challenges or disputes relating to any intellectual property rights owned or used by the Company, including any challenges to the validity, subsistence or ownership of such rights.

7.5.   Please provide details of the Company's Intellectual Property Rights ('IPRs') policies including Internet and security policies and design protocols.

7.6.   Please supply details of any notice(s) or claim(s) that the Company has received or is aware of alleging that the Company has or is alleged to have infringed the IPRs of any third party and, in each case, please provide:

7.6.1.   details of the circumstances of the infringement, alleged infringement, or claim; and

7.6.2.   details of the circumstances surrounding any infringement or claim.

7.7.   Has the Company disclosed to any person any of its intellectual property or other confidential information or trade secrets and if so please provide details and copies of any relevant agreements.

8. Information technology

8.1.   Please supply details of all computer facilities and other information technology hardware or systems (including make, model, specification and capacity) in the possession of and/or used by the Company in the operation of its business and in each case specify which is owned by the Company, which is the subject of any hire purchase, leasing, rental or deferred payment agreement, or which is otherwise provided by a third party.

8.2.   Please supply details of all software (including nature, description, version, and the number of copies licensed) owned or used by the Company.

8.3.   Please supply details of the author of any software owned, or used by, the Company.

8.4.   Please supply copies of all software licences for computer programmes licensed to the Company, any software and new media (including web sites and CD ROMs development, commissioning, hosting and maintenance agreements used by or developed by or on behalf of the Company.

8.5.   Please supply details of any web site operated by or hosted on behalf of the Company and any CD ROMs used by the Company in connection with the Business and the promotion of the Business, and any terms and conditions for the use by third parties of such new media.

8.6.   Please supply a copy of the Company's Data Protection Act Registration and details of the nature of data stored by the Company and whether and to whom such data has been or may be transferred from time to time.

8.7.   Please supply details of:

8.7.1.   any and all of the Company's information technology systems that have been affected by millennium compliance problems or the introduction or use of the ECU and any:

8.7.1.1.   millennium/date compliance ('Y2K') problems; and

8.7.1.2.   problems associated with the introduction and use of ECU.

8.7.2.   the Company's policy and strategy towards the introduction or use of ECU; and

8.7.3.   any audit carried out, or to be carried out, by or for the Company in respect of its information technology systems that are likely to be affected by ECU problems.

9. Directors

9.1.   Please supply the names, addresses and job titles (if any) of each of the directors of the Company and the company secretary and, in each case, specify whether such officer is employed by the Company.

9.2.   Please supply a copy of the service agreement/contract or written statement of terms of employment for each of the officers of the Company and, in each case where there is no such written documentation, please supply details of the officer's:

9.2.1.   obligations and duties;

9.2.2.   length of service;

9.2.3.   date of commencement of service;

9.2.4.   remuneration and fringe benefits (including any accommodation provided);

9.2.5.   unexpired term of office (if employed for a fixed period); and

9.2.6.   details of the notice period required to terminate the officer's employment (on either side).

9.3.   Please supply details of all arrangements between the Company and any of its directors which relate to or affect the capital, business, property, assets or liabilities of the Company and/or any of its group undertakings, and supply copies of all agreements and other documentation relating to the same.

9.4.   Please supply details of all loans granted by the Company and/or any group undertaking to any of the Company's directors, and/or vice versa.

10. **Employees, consultants and sub-contractors**

10.1. Please supply the names of all employees of the Company and in each case specify the employee's position, age, length of service, date of commencement of employment, contractual notice period (on either side), length of any fixed term contracts, salary and other contractual and non-contractual benefits such as entitlement to a bonus, company car, and medical insurance.

10.2. Please supply:

10.2.1. a copy of all standard terms and conditions of employment (if any) for the Company's employees and specify those of the Company's employees to which these are applicable;

10.2.2. details of all employees of the Company who are not employed under the Company's standard terms and conditions of employment and, in each case, supply a copy of the employee's service agreement/contract or if there is no written documentation, supply details of the employee's terms and conditions of employment (including the details set out at 10.1 above);

10.2.3. copies of any staff handbooks and/or circulars;

10.2.4. copies of any disciplinary and grievance procedures;

10.2.5. a copy of any variations to employees contracts which have been notified to employees by means of notice/circular; and

10.2.6. a copy of all current organisation charts.

10.3. Please supply:

10.3.1. the terms of and details of those persons entitled to (together with details of their entitlement) participate in any share option, bonus, incentive or other scheme(s);

10.3.2. details of all bonuses paid out in the last 36 months; and

10.3.3. a copy of any scheme agreements or other documentation relating to the same.

10.4. Please provide:

10.4.1. details of any ex-gratia payments in the last 12 months and of any current or former employees in respect of whom the directors consider the Company to be under a moral or legal obligation to provide retirement or death, accident or sickness disability benefits; and

10.4.2. details of all voluntary pensions or payments and of any current arrangements (whether legally binding or not) for the making of any pension or ex-gratia payments to employees or former employees not covered within the reply to 10.4.1 above, or elsewhere in this questionnaire.

10.5. Please provide details of arrangements to provide paid holiday to each category of employee including calculation of holiday pay.

10.6. Does holiday pay include shift bonuses, overtime payments, performance bonuses or commission payments?

10.7. Please confirm the date upon which the Company's holiday year commences.

10.8. Please confirm the means by which the time worked by each employee, the rest breaks provided and taken by each employee and the holidays taken or holiday pay received, is recorded and in each case please provide an example of the records maintained.

10.9. Please supply details of any job vacancies which are currently, or are about to be advertised and, in addition, details of any job offers made or about to be made.

10.10. Please supply details of any employee absent on sick leave or maternity leave (or who the Company is aware is about to go on maternity leave) or authorised or unauthorised leave of any nature.

10.11. Please supply details of all employees who have resigned or had their employment terminated within the last six months.

10.12. Please supply details of any employee of the Company who has given notice terminating his or her contract of employment or any employee under notice of dismissal.

10.13. If any of the Company's employees work shift patterns, please provide details of the shift patterns worked including start and finish times of each shift, whether the workers perform variable shift patterns, details of rest breaks, daily and weekly rest periods provided and the categories of employees who perform work to shift patterns.

10.14. Please supply details of the systems in place to record compliance with the Working Time Regulations 1998.

10.15. Are there any collective or workforce agreements in place? If yes, please provide full details and copies of all relevant agreements.

10.16. Does the Company have any 'night workers' within the meaning of the Working Time Regulations 1998? If yes, please provide full details.

10.17. Since the Working Time Regulations 1998 came into force on 1 October 1998, has the Company complied with all the Regulations? If not, please provide full details of any breaches.

10.18. Please confirm that all employees who qualify for the national minimum wage have received the national minimum wage since the National Minimum Wage Regulations 1999 came into force on 1 April 1999. If there have been any breaches, please provide full details.

10.19. Please supply details of the systems in place to record compliance with the National Minimum Wage Regulations 1999.

10.20. Please supply copies of any agreement entered into between the Company and any employee in accordance with the National Minimum Wage Regulations 1999.

10.21. Please provide details of all disputes between the Company and any employee or ex-employee, including matters already referred to an Employment Tribunal and those that are expected to be so referred or settled by the payment of money.

10.22. Please supply details of the Company's redundancy policy.

10.23. Please supply the names and addresses of all consultants, sub-contractors or other self employed persons retained/engaged by the Company.

10.24. Please supply a copy of all written agreements with, or written terms of engagement for, all sub-contractors, consultants and self employed persons retained/engaged by the Company, or where there is no written documentation supply details of the terms and condition of retainer/ engagement (including termination provisions).

11. Pensions

11.1. Please supply details of all pension schemes effected by the Company or in which the Company or any of its directors or employees have an interest.

11.2. Please supply a copy of all Trust Deeds and rules (including any amendments).

11.3. Please supply a copy of all explanatory booklets or leaflets distributed to members.

11.4. Please supply a copy of all insurance policies (for insured schemes).

11.5. Please supply a copy of the two most recent valuation reports and details of any actuarial advice or certificates received.

11.6. Please supply a copy of the Trustees' reports and accounts for the last 3 years.

11.7. Please supply details of any special arrangements/augmentations for individual transferees.

11.8. Please confirm that the pension scheme operated by the Company is an Exempt Approved Scheme and, if it is, please confirm that the members of the Company are not aware of any reason why such approval could be withdrawn.

11.9. Please supply a copy of any contracting out certificate.

11.10. Please supply a summary of the deferred and pensioner members of the scheme and a copy of the latest available scheme accounts.

11.11. Please supply a list of the scheme's active members at the annual review date, including their sex, date of birth, pensionable salary and the date upon which each such member joined the scheme.

12. Taxation

12.1. Please supply details to date of tax returns which have been made.

12.2. To what date have tax returns been settled?

12.3. Please supply details of what matters are in dispute or under discussion with the Inland Revenue.

12.4. To what date has tax been deducted under PAYE/VAT and been accounted for and paid over?

12.5. Please supply details of any covenants entered since 6 April 1965 for annual payments of any nature.

12.6. Please supply details of the calculation of deferred tax relating to the last set of audited accounts.

12.7. Please confirm if the Company is, or has been, a 'close company'. If it is or has been, please supply details of any directions which have been made and which are outstanding, including details of any notice of intimation that any direction will be made?

12.8.   Please supply an analysis of the tax provision in the latest accounts with explanation of key components.

12.9.   Please supply copies of the last three years' tax computations.

12.10. Please supply details of any special arrangements with, or dispensations by, any tax authority.

12.11. Please supply details of any overseas trading via non-statutory entities or agents, and details of controls and procedures for compliance with overseas filing requirements.

12.12. PAYE: Please supply a copy of any recent or ongoing audits or investigations in relation to employee taxes and potential exposures in this request.

12.13. VAT: Please supply details of recent or ongoing audits or investigations in relation to VAT, sales taxes and customs duties, and potential exposures in this respect.

13. Properties

13.1.   Please supply details of all property owned by, leased to, licensed to, or otherwise used by the Company, or in which the Company has any interest, and in each case specify:

    13.1.1. the tenure of such property and provide details of areas of both freehold and leasehold title together with plans thereof;

    13.1.2. details of any disputes (including rent reviews and dilapidation claims) subsisting or imminent in relation to any properties;

    13.1.3. registration details.

13.2.   Please supply details of any property transactions in the course of negotiation.

13.3.   Please supply a copy of all survey reports or valuations received by the Company relating to any of the properties owned or occupied by it.

13.4.   Please supply a copy of all title deeds relating to all properties owned by, leased to, licenced or otherwise used by the Company, or in which the Company has any interest.

13.5.   Please supply details of any property, premises or other facilities shared or used in common with other persons and supply a copy of all agreements, licences and other documentation relating to the same.

14. Environmental

14.1.   Please provide details of any land currently or previously owned, occupied, used or held by the Company which is used or has been used (by the Company's previous owners (if any)) for any of the following:

14.1.1.   the deposit or treatment of waste;

14.1.2.   landfilling or backfilling operations;

14.1.3.   any contaminate use which may result in the land being identified as contaminated under section 78B of the Environmental Protection Act 1990; or

14.1.4.   any use requiring a waste disposal licence under Part 11 of the Environmental Protection Act 1990.

14.2.   Please supply copies of any environmental investigations, assessments, reports or audits which the Company has commissioned or which have been carried out in respect of the Company's operations or in respect of any land currently or previously owned, occupied or used by the Company, including any ground investigation surveys.

14.3.   Please supply details (and copies) of all environmental licences relating to the Company.

14.4.   Please provide details of any complaints or prosecutions made or threatened or brought against the Company and any infringements by the Company of any environmental regulations and/or laws including but not limited to:

14.4.1.   the Control of Pollution Act 1974;

14.4.2.   the Water Resources Act 1991;

14.4.3.   the Environmental Protection Act 1990; and

14.4.4.   the Environment Act 1995.

14.5.   Please provide details of any procedures or operations carried out by the Company which involve polluted or contaminated materials.

14.6.   Please provide:

14.6.1.   details of any outstanding recommendations made to the Company by the Environment Agency, the Health and Safety Executive, local authorities or any other statutory body under any environmental or health and safety legislation and regulations;

14.6.2. details of any site at which the Company carries on a process which will require authorisation under Part I of the Environmental Protection Act 1990, including details of whether the relevant process is within Schedule A or Schedule B and whether any indication has been received from the Environmental Agency or the local authority as to any works which the Company will have to undertake in order to obtain authorisation;

14.6.3. details of any complaints or claims by owners or occupiers of any neighbouring land in respect of activities carried on by the Company or in respect of the condition of any land currently or previously owned, occupied, used or held by the Company;

14.6.4. details of any waste disposed of by the Company including the type and amount of waste, examples of transfer notes, consignment notes and registered carriers certificates;

14.6.5. copies of trade effluent consent relating to discharges from any land owned by the Company; and

14.6.6. confirmation that the Company does not need to register under the Producer Responsibility Obligations (Packaging Waste) Regulations 1997.

FINANCIAL DUE DILIGENCE

Since the decision to purchase the business and the price to be paid for it are highly dependent upon the forecast levels of sustainable profit, financial due diligence has long been used to underpin the purchaser's confidence in the figures being talked about. Financial due diligence tends to be historic in focus and is looking at checking underlying performance in the past as a basis for drawing conclusions about the likely achievability of the forecast future performance, together with the current position as regards assets and liabilities.

Accounts, policies, systems and management information

The basic areas that will be reviewed are the company's procedures, systems and policies. Since a company's results are materially affected by the accounting policies adopted, the starting point for most reviews will be the policies to ensure that they meet current **generally accepted accounting practice (GAAP)**. The accountants will be looking to see whether policies adopted appear reasonable in respect of the business (for example depreciating assets such as computers over a sensible lifetime of say three years, calculating the value of stock in an appropriate way, providing for bad and doubtful debts and slow moving stock at appropriate levels given the company's experience, and not anticipating profits before they are earned). In doing so, they will be looking to compare your accounting policies with those generally used in your industry.

They will view the general basis on which your accounts are prepared and how your systems operate in much the same way as will be done during a normal audit to prepare a set of audited financial accounts.

They will want to review the adequacy of the financial information produced and used by the company and you may therefore expect to be asked to produce management accounts, stock reports, aged debtor reports and so on, and to discuss how they are used in the business.

They will therefore be interested in establishing:

- ◆ Is the accounting information adequate to control the business and can the business, for example, demonstrate that it knows the gross margin on a product by product basis or the profitability and cash profile of particular contracts?

♦ Do management demonstrate that they use financial information when making decisions such as investment in plant and equipment or in managing the business?

♦ How widespread is 'financial literacy' within the business?

♦ How integrated is the finance team with operations and sales or does finance appear to operate in isolation?

Profit and loss

Having looked at the systems which produce financial information, they will want to look at detailed trading results on a business unit by business unit basis to review trends in terms of sales, growth margin and overheads to see the degree to which these vary, are seasonal, or differ from the industry average. You will need to be prepared to answer questions about this historic performance as an aid to them in understanding the basis on which future performance is being forecast and how reasonable this appears in the light of prior trading. A forecast going forwards that is broadly in line with past trading trends is going to appear much more reasonable than a forecast that suddenly shows a 50% increase in sales and a 50% increase in gross margin for the same or less level of overhead.

As has already been discussed, this process will be easier if any clutter of non-performing or non-core business has already been disposed of. The due diligence team will be looking to see:

♦ Are there any exceptional items or significant changes or events over the last say three years, which have had an impact on the financial performance of the company? If so what are they? Could they repeat themselves?

◆ Has all the income and expenditure been correctly allocated to the right year, or do the accounts give signs of having been manipulated to show a particular position or trend?

◆ Do the company's contractual relationships seem to make commercial sense in that they are designed to make the company profits based on the costs of its services or products and the risks associated with the contract?

Cash generation

Looking beyond the profit and loss results over the last three years they will look to see what has been the business's ability to generate cash over this period. A statement and source of application of funds can be used to demonstrate where the money has come from and gone to (now known as a cashflow statement). See the example in Figure 8.

◆ Does the company undertake regular cashflow forecasting exercises and does it actively manage its liquidity and effectively chase its debtors?

Overall review of forecasts

They will be asking themselves:

◆ Are the forecast results 'reasonable' based on past performance?

◆ Do the forecast cashflow, profit and loss, balance sheet, and ratios all appear to flow smoothly on from existing trading results, or are there significant changes which require explanation and substantiation?

	£000
Source of funds	
Profit	100
Add back depreciation	<u>50</u>
'Cash' generated from operations	150
Other sources of cash	
Disposal of subsidy	50
Applications of cash	
Investment in plant & equipment	<u>(250)</u>
Net funds used during the period	<u><u>(50)</u></u>
Funded by	
Increase in creditors	(25)
Increase in overdraft	<u>(25)</u>
	<u><u>(50)</u></u>

Figure 8. Example of a simplified statement of source and application of funds.

Assets and liabilities

The current level of assets and particularly liabilities will be reviewed in detail, including:

- **Land and buildings**: are these incorporated at cost or at some later valuation? If so, was this a professional valuation or that of the directors?

- **Plant and machinery and other fixed assets**: how old is plant and machinery? What outstanding hire purchase, finance or operating leases exist? What period are assets being depreciated over (and is this appropriate)? Is the plant and machinery in good condition? How does the estimated value of plant and machinery match up to the book value? There may be need to have an independent valuation of all plant and machinery and property as part of the process.

◆ **Investments**: does the business have any interest in other businesses? If so, what is the nature of the investment and its current value?

◆ **Debtors**: what is the current pattern of aged debtors? What is the history of provision for bad and doubtful debt? Does the company have a significant level of old or disputed debts? Does the company collect in its own debts, or are they collected by a finance house under a factoring arrangement? Does the company appear to have adequate backup in terms of customer orders, copy invoices and proofs of delivery in order to be able to collect old debts?

◆ **Stock and work in progress**: what level of stock is the company holding? How does it divide between raw material stock, work in progress and finished goods stock? How many days/weeks/ months of turnover does the stockholding represent? Does any of the stock appear to be significantly slow moving or obsolete? If so, has it been provided for? On what basis has the stock been valued and does this appear reasonable in relation to the information in the company's accounting system?

◆ **Cash**: they will need a list of all bank accounts held by the company together with the relevant balances, and will review the cashbooks and bank statements for each account over a period for evidence of other bank accounts and for any unusually large transactions that need to be investigated. They will need a file giving lists of the signatories on each account together with the copies of the facility letter, with copies of any security given in respect of borrowings, and details of any balances that have been personally guaranteed by the directors or owners.

♦ Having obtained an aged credit listing they will look to identify the key suppliers, to check that supplier statements have been reconciled, and investigate any unreconciled or disputed items. They will review the process for accruing for expenses where invoices have not been received, and will check the adequacy of the accrual against recent goods received notes and stock records, as well as the level of accruals being carried in respect of utilities and other such overheads.

♦ They will need to obtain a schedule setting out all leases and hire purchase agreements held by the company and showing the balance due and payment schedules. They will also need a list of all potential contingent liabilities from both you and your solicitors which will need to include a list of all outstanding claims and litigation, and they will need to discuss the results with you in some detail.

Obviously in many areas the team undertaking financial due diligence will liaise with the team doing legal and commercial due diligence, for example in the areas of pensions and insurance.

IT
The business's IT systems will be reviewed (both financial and operational) to consider a variety of legal, financial and operational issues, such as:

- Is there a disaster recovery plan in place?

- Does the company have adequate backup security and antivirus protection, and is it licensed to use all its software?

- Is all of the company's data under its own control or does it use third party supplies or outsourcing agreements?

- Does the company's IT infrastructure adequately support the business now and into the future with information and controls or will further investment be required?

Taxation

Past tax computations will be reviewed in detail (together with correspondence with Inland Revenue) to ensure that all tax due has been properly accounted for and dealt with. Treatment of deferred tax will be reviewed and the status of the company as a group or close company will be checked.

If the company has tax losses, the effect of the proposed sale and any changes in the business's ownership and nature of trade will need to be reviewed to see whether these losses can be carried forward and used or will be lost. As part of this review of taxation, the financial due diligence team will be looking to see whether there are any potential tax liabilities which were not otherwise apparent in the accounts.

In addition, compliance with PAYE and VAT regulations and liabilities will be reviewed in detail, checking for any disputes or correspondence with the relevant authorities, filing of returns by the required due dates and absence of any penalties, surcharges or interest.

Sample document – due diligence questionnaire

The following is an example of a standard financial due diligence checklist supplied by Howarth Corporate Finance showing the extent of information and documentation that will typically be requested from the company for sale (the **target**) at the outset of a due diligence process.

Use this and the legal due diligence questionnaire earlier in the chapter as your checklists in advance of any due diligence investigation that you may be subject to in order to ensure that you have everything needed to hand.

Investigations aide mémoire

Information and documents to be requested from the target company

The business

1. History of the company and its business

2. Reports on the company or its products, produced by the company or a third party

3. Recent industry or product surveys

4. Product catalogues and price lists

5. Licensing or distribution agreements

6. Details of the latest order book

7. Copies of agreements with customers

8. Names of any selling agents and summary of goods sold by them. Copies of agency agreements

9. Copies of contracts with suppliers

10. Details of subcontractors and copies of any agreements with them

11. Names of suppliers who sell under Romalpa (reservation of title) clauses

12. Details of disputes with customers or suppliers

13. Details of all patents, trademarks and copyrights granted or applied for showing countries covered

14. Details of all insurance policies

Financial information

1. Last five years' audited accounts

2. Latest management accounts

3. Current budgets, forecasts and cashflow projections

4. Cooperation of the auditor to allow investigating accountants to review audit working papers and tax files

5. Details of all investments in other companies

6. Lists of all motor vehicles owned, leased or hired and users' names

7. Most recent aged listing of trade debtors

8. Schedule of loans made giving details of borrower, authority for loan, amount due, security, interest and repayment terms

9. Most recent aged list of trade creditors

10. Details of all borrowing facilities including security or guarantees given

11. Any financial guarantee or indemnities given to secure credit to third parties

12. Details of charges over assets of the company

13. Copies of all loan agreements

14. Loan capital details; amount, repayment or conversion terms, interest rates, covenants and copies of trust deeds

15. Capital commitments

16. Contingent liabilities

Statutory and legal

1. Details of bankers, lawyers, auditors and any other professional advisors

2. Names of directors and the company secretary and the address of the registered office

3. Memorandum and articles of association

4. Details of shareholders and their shareholdings, and details of all shares

issued

5. Copies of recent directors' minutes

6. Share capital details; options, conversion rights, share incentive or profit sharing agreements and copies of any agreements

7. Copies of all contracts relating to the acquisition or disposal of companies, businesses or fixed assets during the last six years

8. Details of any litigation, actual, threatened or pending

Property

1. Details of premises used by the target giving terms of ownership, location, size, description, dilapidation clauses, rent and rates payable and any recent valuations carried out

2. Copies of leases

3. Copies of any dilapidations schedules served or presented by landlords

4. Details of past payments of rent and rates with a summary of amounts outstanding or prepaid

5. All leases and tenancies granted by the company, details of tenants and terms, assignment of leases where the company was the original lessee

Personnel

1. Details of all staff, including directors, providing age, length of service, salary, benefits (eg car), notice period, department and location. For directors and senior executives CVs and current job descriptions

2. Copies of service agreements, with subsequent amendments, for all directors and senior executives

3. Details of pension or retirement benefits, including a copy of the trust deed and rules, the latest scheme accounts, list of members and actuarial reports

4. Copies of any union agreements

Taxation

1. Copies of last six years' tax computations agreed with the Inland Revenue

2. Details of all matters outstanding with the Inland Revenue

3. Details of latest control visits by PAYE, DSS and VAT authorities and the outcome

4.   Copies of the latest P11Ds and details of benefits in kind

5.   Details of any taxation or Stamp Duty schemes

6.   Copies of any tax clearances obtained or tax indemnities given or taken

Documents supplied by Ward Hadaway and Horwath Corporate Finance

11

Commercial Due Diligence

WHAT AREAS DOES COMMERCIAL DUE DILIGENCE COVER?

Whilst traditional financial due diligence of recent trading performance has always been used as the basis of reviewing forecast trading performance and likely levels of sustained profitability, as in all investment decisions, past performance is not necessarily any guide to future performance. Therefore over recent years, in addition to financial and legal due diligence, increasingly purchasers are undertaking a far more commercially orientated due diligence designed to look at the strategic picture and the business's competitive position within its sector and industry. As such it will be looking at trends within the economy, within the industry, and within the particular market in which the company operates, assessing the company's mix of products and markets, its relationships with key customers and suppliers, its degree of competitive advantage or weakness, and the basis for its existing or potential competitive strategy; many of the areas covered by the business background and market elements of the sales pack discussed in Chapter 7.

In addition to being a vital part of building the purchaser's confidence in your projections of the business, the internal aspects of commercial due diligence are becoming increasingly important for purchasers, as it is increasingly being recognised by purchasers that the success or failure of acquisitions usually depends on how well or poorly the purchaser is able to manage the merging of the acquired company's culture and management into that of their existing organisation (known as **post acquisition integration**).

Research into acquisitions consistently suggests that the majority of acquisitions fail to deliver to the purchaser the value they were expecting to obtain and can therefore be regarded as failures. Further, the research goes on to suggest that in the majority of cases the reason for the 'failure' of the acquisition has nothing to do with the nature of the business being transacted by the target company or any problems crawling out of the numbers after the sale has gone through, but first and foremost is to do with people issues, culture clashes and failure to properly integrate the two businesses so as to achieve the envisaged greater whole.

Alongside the review of the strategic position of the business therefore, the purchaser will be conducting an internal review as to how efficiently the business operates, the quality of its decision making, management culture, and innovation and how these can be expected to integrate with those of the purchaser.

By spending some time during the due diligence process looking at the business's existing structures, culture, and management style, the purchaser can get a much better feel for how they are going to approach dealing with the existing staff and management once the sale has gone through, and can therefore hope to get a much better result going forwards from the sale than otherwise (which will be of particular interest to you if you are on some form of earn-out agreement).

Commercial due diligence involves a review by the purchaser's advisors of three main areas. These are:

◆ **the strategic position**: so as to give the purchaser comfort on the long-term prospects of the business

◆ **the contractual position**: so as to give the purchaser comfort as to the commerciality of the short term position; and increasingly importantly

◆ **people**.

COMMERCIAL AND CULTURE ISSUES CASE STUDY

The accountancy firm Deloitte Haskins & Sells had been founded in the UK in the 1850s by Mr Deloitte and had expanded over the years to become the international firm Deloitte Haskins & Sells, having teamed up with an American accountancy firm in the mid-twentieth century. By the late 1980s it was one of the 'Big Eight' groups of international accountants.

During 1988/89 the partners in the firm, led principally by the US, had decided that in order to remain competitive, they needed to merge with another firm. Driven by the US, the firm decided that its ideal partner was the firm Touche Ross. Discussions were held and eventually an announcement was made to staff that a worldwide merger with Touche Ross was to take place.

The problem with this was that it did not suit all the partners. Whilst the move may have made eminent sense for a variety of strategic reasons for partners in the US, for the partners in various other jurisdictions such as the UK, a local merger with Touche Ross looked distinctly unattractive. As a result, shortly after the announcement that there was to be a worldwide merger with Touche Ross, it became clear that the UK partnership decided it wished to merge with Coopers & Lybrand, a rival accountancy firm, and indeed a number of other local partnerships in other countries took the same view. After a lot of wrangling, the end results of the planned merger with Touche Ross was in fact the breakup of the international firm of Deloitte Haskins & Sells, with much of the firm led by the US merging with Touche Ross, and the bulk of the rest of the firm, led by the UK, merging with Coopers & Lybrand.

Then came the question of the name. Remember the Deloitte, in Deloitte Haskins & Sells had originally come from the UK firm, and not unnaturally the UK firm wished to keep this name in order to maintain its customers in the UK. Meanwhile the American side of the merger regarded the UK and other firms as simply breakaways from the main Deloitte Haskins & Sells business and therefore not entitled to take the name away with them. After a significant period of negotiation, the end result was that:

- Internationally the US firm that had merged with Touche Ross would have the rights to the Deloitte name. Internationally therefore, the new merged entity would be known as Deloitte Touche Tomatsu (where at the same time they had merged with a Japanese firm).

- In the UK however, the UK firm would retain rights to the name for a period of two years and the new merged entity in the UK would for two years be known as Coopers & Lybrand Deloitte. During this two years, the UK firm of Touche Ross which was of course part of the new international partnership Deloitte Touche Tomatsu, would not be allowed to use the name Deloitte and would therefore have to practise as DTT. At the end of two years, Coopers & Lybrand Deloitte would then change its name again, back to Coopers & Lybrand, at which point DTT would be allowed to become Deloitte & Touche in the UK.

I can testify from personal experience that during the first two to three years, and in some cases longer after the merger, much of the partners' energies within the business were given over to internal turf wars over who was to emerge as head of which department, rather than getting out and growing the combined new business. This process carried on down the chain so that it was a good three to four years before members of staff who had come in from each of the preceding partnerships stopped referring to themselves as either 'C' siders or 'D' siders.

This was, I would remind you, the merger of two of the largest accountancy firms in the world, two firms who each provided strategic and corporate finance advice to numerous clients about how to handle business sales, purchases, mergers and post acquisition integration.

It is however a clear example of some of the features that commercial and other due diligence should be picking up to do with:

◆ Intellectual property rights. Who actually owned the Deloitte name?

◆ The strategic sense of the deal for all key staff. Was the proposal going to make sense for all partners and all national firms, and if not, how was the proposed merger planning to bind them in so that there would not be a risk of an embarrassing breakup?

◆ How were the two firms' managements going to be integrated?

◆ How were staff going to be brought in to changing their 'identities' to thinking they were part of one firm?

STRATEGIC REVIEW

To assess the real future prospects of your business, the purchaser needs to understand:

- The big 'external' forces affecting your industry and business and what **opportunities and threats** arise from this by understanding:
  - What is happening in the business environment? ('PEST' analysis – see below).
  - What forces are shaping the structure of your industry and how much money can be made in it? (Industry structure or Porter's Five Forces – see below).

- Your business's 'recipe' and its **strengths and weaknesses**.
  - What products are you supplying into which markets and what potential growth strategies are there?
  - Where are your products in their lifecycles and have you got an appropriate portfolio of products?
  - What do your customers want?
  - What is your competitive advantage (based on what your customers want) within your industry on which you can build?
  - What is your unique selling proposition?

What trends affect your industry? ('PEST' analysis)

The world is a changing place. Developments across a range of factors will have an impact on your industry or business. So the purchaser's advisors will be asking: 'What are the major trends in the business environment in which you are operating that will affect your industry and business?'

There are five main headings that need to be considered for any industry, which can be summarised in a table as:

Politics/legislation	◆ Requirement for all widget users to be licensed from next year ◆ EU widget standard announced ◆ Privatisation of French state owned widget manufacturer
Economics	◆ Coming out of recession, long-term growth expected ◆ Widget raw material prices will rise ◆ Growth of industrial widget users slowing ◆ Direct selling of widgets taking off
Social	◆ Demand for recyclable widgets ◆ Domestic widgets becoming fashionable
Technological	◆ Digital widgets to become commercially viable within two years
Industry realignment	◆ European and US widget makers entering UK market and purchasing small UK manufacturers

Figure 9. PEST analysis.

The purchaser will be looking to establishing how the impact of these factors is going to change your industry over the foreseeable future, and how your business needs to change to meet any threats arising (eg a need to invest) or opportunities opening up (eg new markets or an opportunity to sell the business).

How is your industry structured? (Porter's Five Forces)

The attractiveness of any industry and the potential to make significant profits tend to be governed by the interaction of a number of forces. These will be analysed by asking you the five key questions as set out in Figure 10.

What products do you sell into which markets?

Your business will have a 'portfolio' of products and markets. The starting point for assessing the opportunities for future growth is by way of a product/market ('Ansoff') matrix as shown in Figure 11. This sets out a basic matrix for your business by asking two questions:

What will keep other people out of your industry? (Barriers to entry)

Requirement for:

◆ regulation/licensing
◆ high investment required in capital/brand building
◆ high economy of scale/learning curves
◆ restricted access to distribution channels or technology

will mean it is dicult for newcomers to enter the industry and threaten prices (eg how easy is it to set up a new airline?)

Who has more power, you or your → supplier?

Where there are:

◆ few suppliers and many buyers
◆ differentiated products
◆ no satisfactory substitute

this will mean the supplier's negotiating power is high (eg Heinz ketchup)

How intense is competition within the industry?

The existence of:

◆ high 'exit' barriers
◆ lack of differentiated product
◆ high fixed costs
◆ industry overcapacity

will imply intense competition and price pressure (eg how high are margins in the petrol refining part of the industry?)

What substitute products are there?

The existence of:

◆ high rates of legislation or technological change
◆ low switching costs for consumers
◆ high savings from new products
◆ fashion changes

will mean that new alternative products can rapidly replace existing suppliers (eg how secure in the long term is any computer software or hardware business?)

Who has more power, you or your customer?

Where there are:

◆ a few buyers and many sellers
◆ commodity products
◆ the buyer controls distribution channels
◆ the buyer has low switching costs between suppliers

will mean that the customer will tend to have the whip hand (eg who has the power, supermarkets or most of their suppliers?)

Figure 10. The key questions of Porter's five forces.

What products do you supply?	What markets/customer groups distribution channels do you supply?			
	Direct to the public mail order	Small UK shops	UK supermarkets	New channel
Widgets	✓	✓	—	X
Thingamies	✓	✓	✓	
Servicing	—	✓	✓	
New product	Y			Z

Figure 11. SA product/market ('Ansoff') matrix.

The due diligence team will then look to home in on each area to understand:

♦ What is the size of each product market box (segment) as a potential market?

♦ How much do you sell into this box (your 'share')?

♦ Is the market demand in that segment growing, steady or declining?

They will then explore the potential of the four basic growth strategies for any business which are then (in normal order of ease/risk):

(i) **Improving market penetration** by boosting sales to your existing customers who already know you and your products:

♦ Looking for the **gaps** – UK supermarkets (existing customers) are not taking any widgets (an existing product). Why not? What can be done to change this?

- Increasing your **share of a channel** – do you supply 1%, 10% or 100% of small UK shops' demand for widgets? How can your share of that customer/market's spend on this type of product be increased?

(ii) **Developing new customers and markets** for existing products, such as widgets (**box X**):

- Can existing customers be persuaded to refer new customers to the company by incentivising them?

- Can new types or groups of customers be identified who you can sell to? (eg business A might be a potential supplier to garage chains or overseas distributors.)

(iii) **Developing new products** based on your existing core skills to sell to your existing customers to meet their other needs (**box Y**), particularly those of the acquiring company. Is there scope to add on a widget rental business, or becoming the UK licensee of the new Italian 'Gadgetti'?

(iv) Finally, and most risky of all, there is **diversification (box Z)** – the potential to develop a new product for supply to a new set of customers. This is regarded as highly risky because it involves developing a new product about which you have no knowledge, and selling it into a new market where you have little existing credibility as potential customers do not know you.

The acquirers will be looking to see how to achieve most from each of the above strategies, which will involve focusing on the most attractive product/market segments, which are those:

- with high growth

◆ where you make high profits
◆ where you have the most strength on which to grow.

Where are your products in their lifecycle and do you have an appropriate portfolio?
Individual products will have a lifecycle such as that in Figure 12 in which they either eventually fade away, are overtaken by newer products, or have to be reinvented. This process can take many years (the ocean liner) or be extremely fast (this year's fashion).

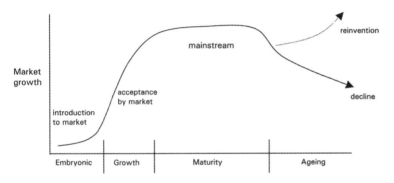

Figure 12. A product lifecycle.

New products tend to eat cash in development and marketing in order to grow their market share, before becoming established and generating surplus cash.

The Boston Consulting Group matrix (shown in Figure 13) is used to look at managing a portfolio of products (or businesses).

The purchaser will be looking to see where in the matrix your products are, you have an appropriate balanced portfolio of up and coming, as well as established, products, or are all the businesses establsihed cash cows or new question marks?

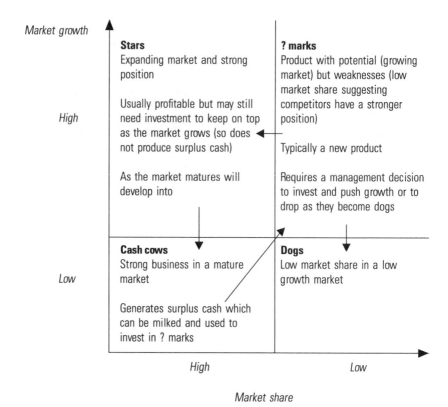

Figure 13. The Boston Consulting Group Matrix.

What do your customers want (critical success factors)?

There will be different things that are important to your customers in making their decisions about who to buy from.

◆ These are things that all potential suppliers must have/be able to do to be considered, known as **order qualifiers** – which airline will fly me from Heathrow to New York?

◆ And then there are things that decide which of the potential suppliers is actually chosen, or **order winners**, such as which airline will offer the best seats, food and frequent flier programme.

The purchaser's advisors may ask management to rank the importance of these factors on a scale of 0–10 as Company A has done below, together with how management thinks (or better still if the information is available, how customers think) its own performance and its competitors' performance rates.

Critical factors	Importance to customers 0–10	Company's performance	Competitors B	C	D
Price	6	7	3		
Quality	9	6	10		
Range	4	10	5		
Service backup	8	9	10		
Speed of delivery	3	5	1		

Figure 14. Critical success factors.

The acquirer will be looking to see why these factors are important to your customers, and what needs customers are satisfying in buying from you. The purchaser is looking for comfort as to why customers want to buy your product at all. This is important as customers purchase to achieve benefits (of the ability to have a hole when they need one) rather than features (this drill is made of high speed steel). So to ensure that your business has a long-term future, buyers will want comfort that your marketing addresses how customers' needs are met by your service (often emotional), *not* on its features (often technical).

What is your competitive advantage?

The long-term success that the purchaser is looking for relies on establishing and maintaining a 'competitive advantage' (A) over your present and future competitors. This can be quickly summarised as:

$$\frac{A = (B, C, D) \times W^K - X}{£N}$$

This means that you have a successful recipe for doing things

- better (B), cheaper (C) or differently (D) from your competitors;
- in a way that customers want (W)
- and know about (K),
- which competitors cannot copy (X – for Xerox),
  which overall makes money now (£N). And then keeping it successful (so that it remains based on what customers want and is not copied). If you can demonstrate a strong recipe of this type as set out on a simple table such as the one below, this provides a compelling story to form the basis of the purchaser's confidence in the long-term health of the business.

This sort of competitive advantage has to be underpinned by well developed business strengths in a variety of areas, the key ones being:

- **Reputation** – for many products it is often very difficult (eg from brain surgery to motor oil) to inspect the quality of the goods prior to purchase, so many customers will rely on brand names and reputation as a 'safe choice', even if this means paying a premium.

- **Strategic assets** – where investing in gaining dominance in a narrow niche (eg left-handed widgets) or in capital equipment, economies of scale, sewing up the key suppliers or distribution networks, know-how and improved skills from learning curve effects, can give a significant long-term advantage over competitors (and therefore certainty for the purchaser).

What do you do that is:		Why does this matter to customers?	Can this be copied?
Better in a way that customers can identify and perceive as delivering extra value	Well respected brand name for quality and service	Trusted for quality	Only with years of investment
Cheaper for you to do than your competitors	Through better innovation, automation and waste management we manufacture at 25% less than our competitors	We can sell cheaper than our competitors	Partly, would require major investment in machinery, but it would be difficult to replicate our know-how
Different that specifically meet the needs of particular groups of customers	We make the only left-handed widget	Left-handed people find right-handed widgets very awkward	Yes, but it's a small market and probably not worth anyone else investing in the machinery

Figure 15. Competitive advantage summary.

- The ability to successfully and commercially innovate and develop new and better ways of doing things or products and services can give you an advantage over your competitors (but you also need to be able to manage the risks associated with innovation and keep the key staff involved in innovation, and keep them committed to the business after the sale).

- **Internal organisation and infrastructure** – such as efficient stock and wastage control or internal communication which make you more efficient than your competitors.

- **External networks** can also help, such as joint venture and strategic alliances, or membership of a purchasing ring.

Do you have the right value chain?
What really makes your business worth buying is:

- what really makes your business different from any other in your industry (your unique selling proposition – USP), and

- that you have set up your business to really commit to delivering that proposition to customers (your value chain).

For a business set up to deliver 'the lowest cost widget', the purchaser will be looking to see that all aspects of your organisation and strategy are set up to deliver this to your customers as illustrated in Figure 16.

WHY CULTURE MATTERS

Case study
I was in involved in discussions over the potential merger of two mid-sized professional firms.

Firm A, based in the City of London, had a very plush, well appointed and neat reception area, with well tended plants and very tidy displays of corporate material. I was taken to meet the senior partner in his well appointed office, and everyone we passed in the corridors was wearing a smart, conservative business suit.

At firm B, a larger (and more profitable practice) based in the West End of London, with a reputation for handling an entrepreneurial client base, I waited in a decidedly scruffy metal-floored, mezzanine

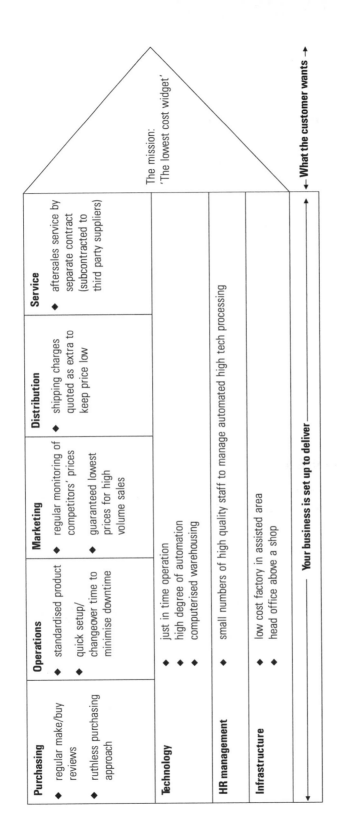

Figure 16. Business value chain.

reception area with magazines and papers scattered on the desk and a definite air that the cleaner was due in tomorrow for their weekly stint. Meanwhile staff in open-necked shirts came into reception to greet clients and I was eventually shown into a meeting room with boxes of records stacked in a corner and joined by the senior partner, dressed in chinos and a sports jacket and carrying a mug of coffee.

In many ways the commercial and geographical fits of the two organisations were very good. The truth was however, that due to the cultural differences between the firms, it was already apparent that any attempted merger stood little real chance of success.

Some of the strongest forces operating within your business are its culture and structure, but because they have grown up over time, have never been formally set out, and form such a pervasive background of 'how we do things here', the wood is often all but invisible to those working inside the business (including you), who only see trees. But they are vital to prospective purchasers as they are probably the key difference between a successful or failed acquisition.

Your business's culture and structure are different but linked as shown below.

Culture	Structure
The shared values, experience and beliefs of the business that set out how we do things here:	How the business is organised:
◆ independent of management	◆ set by management
◆ informal	◆ formal
◆ war stories, in-jokes, reputations, myths	◆ public (eg organisation charts)

Figure 17. Culture and structure.

As businesses develop in size and complexity, the cultural style and the structure often develop along parallel lines from a power to role culture and from entrepreneurial to a functional structure.

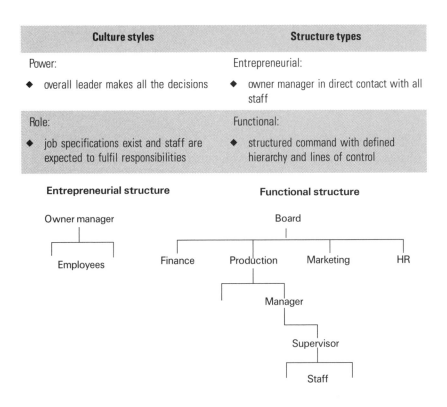

Culture styles	Structure types
Power:	Entrepreneurial:
◆ overall leader makes all the decisions	◆ owner manager in direct contact with all staff
Role:	Functional:
◆ job specifications exist and staff are expected to fulfil responsibilities	◆ structured command with defined hierarchy and lines of control

Figure 18. Culture and structure types.

Mapping the organisation

In reviewing your culture and organisation, the purchaser's advisors will need to:

◆ Draw an organisation chart showing who formally reports to whom. How clearly structured is it? How logically organised is it?

◆ Review to what extent this 'formal structure' reflects the reality and the lines of power which relate to who goes to whom for decisions. Does this follow the 'formal structure'? If not, why not? (For example, Fred is the factory manager, but all the lads on the shop floor still come to you as 'the boss' for all the decisions.)

◆ Everyone on the chart will need to be given a job title. Do they make sense given the lines drawn above?

◆ Check who is responsible for each of the key roles in your business (such as sales, marketing, customer services, purchasing, production, despatch, quality control, research and development, finance, personnel, overall strategic direction and drive).

Assessment of the management team

Having identified the key individuals, the purchaser will need to assess how strong the team is and how to ensure that those members of the team that are critical to the business's future success are tied into the business.

Increasingly, psychometric tests form a key part of such management assessments and some useful psychometric tests can be ordered on line at www.turnaroundhelp.co.uk.

This work can be critical to the purchaser in planning their post acquisition integration strategy; their plan as to how they are going to manage the process following the sale, of integrating their newly acquired business into their own existing organisation and make any changes that they plan to make. An example of the areas such an assessment of management might want to cover is set out on the next page.

Person	Fred	George
Role	Production Manager	Accountant
Qualification	Engineering degree	'By experience'
Experience and industry knowledge	Seven years with Widget Inc as line manager	Company accountant and bookkeeper since 1956
Ability to think strategically	Limited, very much a 'nuts and bolts' man, internally focused	A bookkeeper's bookkeeper
Financial awareness	Focused on cost management. Can read a P&L	None, a number cruncher, not a manager
Team type	Driver, comes up with a plan, ensures it is seen through. Good evaluator and completer-finisher	Solitary worker
Personality type	Goal orientated, practical. Reserved with people, works in a structured way	Jobsworth. Poor communicator. No imagination
Record of delivery	Strong within own sphere	Produces numbers but unable to help manage finances
Experience of bad times?	Yes, two-year slump at Widget Inc	None
Willingness to change	Will change once works through for himself that change is needed	Dislikes change
Commitment to company and plan/interest in outcome	Appears loyal and strongly committed	Retiring in two years
Critical to business?	Yes	No
Attitude to sale	Positive	Negative
Strategy		

Figure 19. Management assessment.

12

The Sales Contract and Completion

THE TWIN TRACK PROCESS

Negotiation of the sales contract will take place at the same time as the purchaser is carrying out their due diligence. Detailed negotiations will therefore proceed side by side with information that the purchaser is obtaining as part of their due diligence process which will then feed in to their views on the overall price, terms of the deal, and specific promises made about the business, the representations and warranties which may have a cost implication by way of indemnities and covenants that they may wish to have incorporated in to the contract.

Having agreed heads of terms, it is important from your point of view as the seller, to ensure that the whole process of completing the due diligence and negotiation of the final sales contract proceeds as quickly as possible. The longer a deal goes before closure, the more likely it is to fall apart as a result of a variety of events such as outside elements changing, the buyer getting cold feet, an alternative better proposition coming along, the person pushing your deal at their end changing jobs, leaves, is given the boot, or news leaks out of the deal which adversely affects the business.

Having reached this stage, do not let a deal slip away from you by simply letting the process run out of steam. You and your advisors will need to keep pressure on the buyer to complete the deal within the time frame discussed. Remember, one of the points of including a specified exclusivity period in the heads of terms is so that the purchaser knows that if they do not do the deal within the term specified, they are again open to competition.

THE SALES CONTRACT

The sales contract is the legally binding document which, once signed, sets out the contract for sale, specifying the assets that are sold, the price, the terms of payment, the effective date, and the conditions under which the sale will actually be concluded which is usually but not always simultaneously on exchange of contracts. To protect the purchaser from agreeing to buy something that is apparently worth £X at one date and completing the sale at whatever the effective date is some time later only to find that the business is now worth £Y, any sale agreements relating to a deferred completion date will specify conditions that have to be met for the sale contract to be valid at the time of completion, such as no loss of a specified list of key customers, turnover continuing to run at a specified level, or net assets not having fallen below a specified level.

In addition, and probably more crucially, the sales contract sets out the representations, warranties, covenants, and indemnities that will define where and how risk lies in the deal with the buyer and the seller (and those in respect of tax may be codified into a separate tax indemnity agreement in a share sale). It is over the nature and wording of these areas that much of the discussion in drawing the deal to a conclusion will take place and where you need a sharp, experienced legal advisor acting on your behalf to ensure that you achieve the deal you think you have.

The sales contract is usually drafted by the buyer's solicitor and if they do so, it will be on the basis that they are acting to protect their client, the purchaser. The first draft you receive is therefore likely to contain quite onerous representations, warranties, and covenants for you to agree to, together with potentially ruinous indemnities, and possibly contractual points and arrangements which weren't actually what you had thought you had agreed with the purchaser.

Once you have recovered from the shock, remember that this is the starting point and the object of the exercise will be to negotiate to a mutually acceptable set of terms for the sale.

It is worth taking a step back to understand what the particular problem is with the sales contract. This arises from a fundamental conflict of interest between the buyer and the seller. As a seller, you are seeking certainty about what you have sold your business for, and you are therefore looking to protect the value that you believe you require for the deal. Ideally therefore, you would like a sales contract that says: 'I [the purchaser] will pay you [the seller] £X for the business.'

However, the buyer is looking for certainty about what they have bought. They are therefore looking to protect the value of what they have bought against any problems that subsequently arise, which had they known them at the time, would have affected the amount of money they were prepared to pay for your business. Therefore from the purchaser's point of view, they would like a sales contract that says: 'We [the purchaser] will buy the business from you [the seller] for £X, less any amounts by which the value of the business once we are in charge of it, falls short of the expectations we had before we took it over.'

The difference between these two positions of an outright certain value on the one hand and a value that is completely contingent on future performance and whether the business matches up to expectations on the other, is dealt with by way of the sharing of risk through the representations, warranties, and indemnities (and to a certain extent covenants).

So what are representations, warranties, indemnities and covenants?

A representation is any statement made to the purchaser about the business. This may be in discussion, by way of answers to questions about due diligence, or in connection with a formal disclosure letter which is a document prepared as part of the answers to due diligence questions in connection with the negotiation of the sales contract that sets out specific facts about the business. In some cases the **disclosure letter** is specifically incorporated into the sales contract as a schedule; in other cases it may simply be referenced. A disclosure letter should give all the relevant facts in respect of any particular item covered, the emphasis being upon *all*. Whilst it is up to the purchaser to draw the relevant conclusions from any particular set of facts, the full facts around any circumstance known to the seller should be mentioned.

Since the sales process will last for a prolonged period and the purchaser will deal with a large range of individuals within the seller's organisation and advisors, in practice, you have very little control over the full range of representations that have been made to the purchaser during the presale process, or due diligence. You therefore run a real risk that at some point during discussions some employee may, innocently or otherwise, have said something to the purchaser or their advisors which may subsequently give rise to a problem. Therefore, to protect yourself against this, you need to seek to include an 'entire agreement' clause setting out that the purchaser has not relied upon any representations (written or oral) except for those that are specifically stated as being incorporated into the agreement, which in practice will be those given in the disclosure letter.

A warranty is a guarantee that the particular facts are as they are stated to be. During the process of precontractual negotiations and then due diligence, the purchaser will have gathered a huge number of representations either written or oral about the nature of the company's business, its trading and its assets and liabilities. Obviously these will all feed into their understanding of what the business is worth to them. What they will seek to do by use of both the disclosure letter and by warranties, is to get comfort as to those specific matters that are most important to them as the basis on which to value the business. Therefore, the purchaser will be looking for the key points on which they have made the decision to buy the business to be confirmed to them by way of warranties since this gives the purchaser protection that if these facts turn out not to be right, they have some comeback against you to seek what is in practice a discount on the price they have paid. The use of warranties also forces you to ensure that you have been accurate and thorough in providing them with accurate information as only if you provide them with accurate information in the disclosure letter, will you be protected from any action concerning misrepresentation.

A warranty is therefore a contractual term and should the term of that warranty be breached, then you as the seller are in breach of the contract and the buyer can claim against you for damages. In order to do so they are going to need to be able to demonstrate that:

- the warranty was actually specifically breached

- this breach was not excluded by way of specific disclosure in the disclosure letter, and

- the breach results in a specific and quantifiable reduction of the value of the business against what has been paid.

While the buyer may have a general claim against you for a breach of warranty, the value of this may vary and will need to quantify the damages to be sought in respect of the circumstances giving rise to the breach of warranty. An indemnity by contrast is a guaranteed specific recompense to the purchaser in respect of a particular breach. Therefore whilst in general if you breach a warranty, the purchaser has to prove that the breach has damaged the value of the business in order to chase you for money, if you breach an indemnity, the seller has a specific remedy against you even if the value of the business remains unchanged.

An indemnity will therefore usually seek a £1 to £1 remedy for specific loss incurred as a result of a specific liability arising and will be used, for example, in respect of tax liabilities, where the sales contract may specify that the expected tax liability of the business is £X. In the event that it is more than £X, this amount can be clawed back from the seller.

Example of how the terms interact

A set of disclosures, representations, warranties and indemnities might operate as follows:

Warranty	There are no claims against the company in respect of defective widgets except as disclosed in the disclosure letter.

Disclosure letter	As at the date of the sales contract, the company has two claims against it in respect of malfunctioning widgets. Mr Smith, who is claiming £10 and Mr Bloggs, who is claiming £20.
Indemnity	In the event of any claims being received by the company following the date of sale in respect of malfunctioning widgets sold prior to the date of sale, the seller will reimburse the purchaser the full amount of any settlement made to the complaining customer.

Therefore, the warranty sets out the specific issue being addressed and the comfort being given by the company. The disclosure letter sets out the detail of any exceptions to the general comfort being given, and the indemnity sets out a specific basis upon which the purchaser can claim against the seller in the event that the warranty turns out not to be true and the company receives a claim from Mr Jones for £30 in respect of malfunctioning widgets.

Figure 20.   Interaction of warranty, disclosure letter and indemnities.

As indemnities have to be very tightly specified, they are usually much more narrowly drawn than general warranties, and limited in nature. Whilst the best sales contract is without doubt one that once signed is filed and is never seen or used by either the purchaser or the seller ever again, it is therefore important to realise how the purchaser will be looking to use warranties in order to confirm their certainty as to what they are buying. From this point of view, to the degree that warranties give the buyer certainty as to what they are buying, warranties are in your interests because the more certain they are about what they are buying, the higher price they will be prepared to pay for your business. At the same time however, that certainty is coming at the price of your uncertainty as to your final outcome as it gives the purchaser recourse back to you in the event that things do not work out and the purchaser finds that what they have bought does not correspond to what they thought they were buying, or how they thought it would perform.

The purchaser will be looking therefore to establish:

◆ what warranties they need to have in place to confirm the facts upon which they have decided to buy the business

◆ what indemnities they need to have in place in order to ensure they are covered against foreseeable problems or liabilities

◆ under what circumstances might a breach of the warranties be so serious that they might want to write to rescind the contract

◆ as well as practical issues to do with how do they establish the breach, what is their procedure for claiming damages, should some money be set aside in an escrow account for a period, so as to provide them something to go at if they need to claim for warranties or breaches, is their scope to claim warranties open ended, both in terms of time and value?

Conversely as the seller you will need to seek to ensure that the warranties and indemnities given are as limited as possible, that the disclosure letter fully sets out items which could otherwise give rise to some claim for breach of warranties, as well as ensuring that there are restrictions as to the maximum overall level of any claims, a limit on individual claims, a limit as to the time under which claims can be made, and a limit as to type of claims, so that items other than those specifically included in the sales contract cannot be claimed for.

Whilst therefore you will generally want to sell on an as-seen basis (or the only two words of Latin most accountants know, *caveat emptor* – buyer beware), you are unlikely to be able to insert into any sales contract a clause that says that the purchaser has relied solely upon their own enquiries in forming a view as to whether to buy.

You will typically need to agree a number of basic warranties about the state of the business and its affairs such as (subject to any exceptions disclosed in the disclosure letter):

- that the tax returns have been filed and payments are up to date

- that the financial statements fairly and accurately represent the company's position and current performance

- that there is no pending or existing litigation against the company

- that the company's assets belong to it, it has full title to all its assets and properties, and there are no encumbrances or security granted over the company or its assets

- there are no undisclosed liabilities

- that the company is meeting relevant Health and Safety, and employment regulations

- that the company has all the licences necessary to operate within its business, and is not in breach of any regulations

- that there are no notices served to terminate any leases or contracts, or

- that all the company's intellectual property is the property of the company and not of individuals within the company.

In discussing any warranties that the purchaser requires, you will obviously have to balance your desire not to give a warranty so as to limit your risk and therefore increase your certainty as to the amount of money you walk away with, versus the degree of suspicion and concern that refusal to give a specific warranty may cause a buyer.

Assuming that the sales contract will include indemnities and warranties, as a seller you will need to ensure that you manage your exposure to these. Therefore, together with your legal advisor, you need to ensure that the sales contract builds in protection for you in how and to what extent a claim can be made. As far as possible you should seek to:

♦ Limit the duration of the period under which any claim can be brought to a specific period, say one or two years or until completion of the first full year audit after the sale as you would expect that within that time, if there was anything untoward in what you have said to the purchaser, they should by now have uncovered it. At the same time, match this period with a period under which any money is held back in an escrow account is to be released to you. The purpose of holding money in an escrow account is to allow the purchaser to have some certainty that, should they need to make a claim on you, there is money to meet it.

♦ Limit the total amount to which you are exposed to a percentage of the sales value so that the whole of the proceeds you have acquired are not at risk. Given that in coming to complete the sales contract the purchaser will have done their due diligence, it is not unreasonable to seek to limit the total amount of their claim to only, say, 20%, 30% or even 50% of the sales price as they will have had the opportunity to undertake significant enquiries.

♦ Avoid being bothered by lots of small claims as it is likely that in any sales contract, there may well be a myriad of small technical breaches of warranties or indemnities, depending upon how widely these are drawn, and you do not want to have to deal with lots of small claims by the purchaser. One technique for managing this is to have a minimum threshold which either individual claims or a basket of claims before they will be dealt with, on the basis that a number of small claims are not worth bothering about.

◆ Avoid having too much of your money tied up in an escrow account. Ensure that only a percentage is there, say up to 20% of the sales price, and that the account is interest bearing with the interest payable to you, the period limited to the length of any claims period and, if possible, the money released to you in stage payments.

Obviously if part of the sales price is being paid by way of an earn-out, the call by the purchaser for some form of escrow account can be discounted, since in effect the deferred payment/earn-out will act as the escrow account.

COVENANTS

There are two types of covenants involved in a sale which can loosely be described as precompletion and postcompletion.

Precompletion covenants relate to your promises as to how you will manage the business in any period between exchange of contracts and completion of the sale. You will generally be required to sign a covenant that you will manage the business in such a way that there are no major changes in its legal structure, financial arrangements or its basic trading patterns, and that you will not make major changes to the company, take on major new debt, or sell assets.

The other major covenant is a postcompletion covenant where, in almost all sales, the seller will have to sign a non-competition agreement. This may either be part of the main sales contract or may occasionally be a separate contract with you as an individual for which there will then be separate payment. A non-competition covenant will be used to prevent you as the seller competing with the company once it has been sold. Buyers will generally insist on this as they want to protect their investment in the intangibles of the business they have bought, including the know-how, the contacts with customers, the relationships with key suppliers, and so on.

While courts will enforce properly drawn up non-competition covenants, particularly where there has clearly been specific consideration offered by the purchaser and accepted by you for giving this covenant, there is also a general principle that you have a right to earn a living. Therefore the courts will look at any non-competition covenant and only allow it to be enforced where it is fairly specific in terms of a geographical area, a period and an activity which you agree not to compete in. So a very widely drawn non-competition covenant may in fact be unenforceable by the purchaser. In practice this is always a negotiating point where the buyer will generally want to have a fairly wide non-competition clause and the seller may wish a more narrow one so as to keep their options open. But this then becomes a matter for you to consider depending upon your objectives coming out of the sale. For example, if you are not actually intending to compete in this area with the seller going forwards, then this represents a negotiating point you can trade with the purchaser for the sake of other concessions. Bear in mind however, that if you negotiate too hard in terms of not wishing to sign a non-competition covenant, you may raise suspicions in the mind of the purchaser that you are intending to

compete once the deal has been finalised, which may raise
uncertainty about the value of the business they are buying.

NON-EMBARRASSMENT CLAUSE

How would you feel if you sold your business (or shares in it) to
someone for, say, £500,000, only to find that they went out and sold
it on again to someone else shortly afterwards for £1m?

This situation can be avoided by use of a non-embarrassment clause
whereby the purchaser agrees to pass on a specified share of any
sales proceeds in excess of the price paid in the original sale, in the
event of a subsequent sale within a specified time period. It is usual
to seek to include this type of clause in a sale to fellow shareholders
or family members.

CLOSURE

Once the sales contract has been signed and exchanged, there may in
some cases then be a period between exchange and completion. This
sometimes comes as a surprise to sellers but in practice, where a
buyer is buying with finance they are raising from other sources, it
may well be that final release of their funds is dependent upon the

bank or finance company having sight of the contract or regulatory approval may be required. There may therefore be a period of, say, two or four weeks, between exchange and the proposed date of completion.

The way in which you manage the business in the period between exchange and completion will be covered by way of covenants that you will give as discussed above. In order to protect the purchaser from buying a business that has suffered severe deterioration between the date of exchange and the date of completion, the sales contract will also specify the conditions that must be met for the contract to be completed, again as set out above. The date of completion will be the day on which all documents are completed and funds are formally transferred. In practice completion day is often hectic, involving a large amount of work for advisors for both companies. Legal teams will be involved in ensuring documents of title to assets or share transfers are passed across and that funds have been received into the right bank accounts in the right amount at the correct times. At the same time, valuers may well be on site undertaking an inventory of fixed plant and equipment, and a stock count, while accountants may be involved in doing cut-off tests on debtors and creditors so as to be able to quickly draw up completion accounts showing the trading performance in the last set of accounts to the date of transfer.

Since there is so much to be finalised, particularly in terms of transferring legal documents, it is vital that if not undertaken as part of preparation for due diligence in the period leading up to the actual date of completion, all legal documentation (including such paperwork as intellectual property rights, trademarks, and patents) is reviewed and readied for transfer. The last thing you want to see when you have accountants, valuers, and surveyors running all over your business, is to find there is some hitch in terms of some particular document of title or trademark documentation that causes a problem in completing the deal. At the same time, you need to agree with the purchaser the communication strategy for announcing the deal to your workforce, your customers, suppliers, the press and any other interested parties. The day of closing will be a very busy, long, and stressful affair, and you should do as much preparation as possible to ensure processes go as smoothly as possible and avoid any last minute surprises. At this moment more than any other, unpleasant surprises can really jeopardise deals, as it is the purchasers' last chance to change their minds.

GOLDEN RULE 20

Expect to have to offer training or consultancy to the purchaser
Having built the business up, much of the knowledge about how it works, its know-how and its customer relations will inevitably reside in your head. In order to obtain value from the business, the purchaser is going to need to have you transfer that knowledge, skills, know-how, introductions, contacts and so on across to them as the new owner of the business. This may require you to stay on to give a short period of training over a few weeks in how the business operates, or to stay on for a longer period of say, two years, to act as a consultant introducing the new owners to the customers and gradually handing over these relationships.

As we have seen, the more that you can incorporate this knowledge into your business, such that it does not rely on you and can clearly operate as a stand alone business, the less reliance the purchaser has to put on you and your cooperation following a sale and therefore the higher the price they are willing to be able to pay, but also the less call there is going to be on you going forwards. Of course as we have also seen, it may be that as part of the price negotiations and the terms of the deal, you may wish to have an extensive period of consultancy in order to manage your tax affairs.

But eventually it will all be over, you will have heard from the solicitor that the money has been transferred by wire transfer and has been received into the relevant bank account, that all the documentation has been dealt with, transferred to the purchaser, and it is time to open that bottle of champagne and start the postdeal party.

SAMPLE DOCUMENT – A TYPICAL SHARE PURCHASE AGREEMENT

As you will have seen from this chapter, the key issues to be looking out for are how you are being asked to take the risk in the sale, both by the extensive warranties that are suggested, but also by the absence of protection of your sales proceeds. This is the time when having an experienced corporate finance lawyer fighting your corner is invaluable.

Document health warning

It should be stressed that the document that follows which has been summarised from an example by Ward Hadaway is included only for the purposes of illustration. It is not intended to be used as a comprehensive legal 'precedent' and accordingly does not contain all the clauses which might be desirable from the point of view of either a buyer or a seller. Instead it is intended to represent the final form of purchase document that might typically be reached after a full negotiation process has been followed between a buyer and seller of roughly equivalent bargaining power. As a result the example contains compromises on a number of issues and also omits clauses which could be construed as having a high degree of either buyer or seller bias.

It is also not tailored to any particular factual situation and includes general provisions relating to intellectual property, freehold and leasehold property, environmental regulation and pensions issues which might affect any particular transaction. If any of these, or other, specialist areas are of importance in respect of a particular deal, then the focus of the real documentation will change and more detailed warranties will be included.

In a contract for a purchase of business and assets, the terms will define what particular assets are to be purchased and which liabilities are to be assessed, together with specific matters such as whether the sale is on the basis of a sale as a going concern and how VAT is to be dealt with.

The attachment is a summary of a draft on a clause by clause basis, the original document running to 85 pages of A4. Even in summarised form however, this should provide you with an indication of the scale and depth of documentation required, particularly in dealing with the issues surrounding warranties.

As with all legal documents, actual agreements should only be drafted by professional advisors sufficiently qualified and experienced to understand all the issues arising from them, and from any particular factual situation. You should always seek specific advice for all specific situations and neither the author, the publisher, Ward Hadaway or Howarth Corporate Finance who have kindly supplied the sample documents, cannot accept any responsibility for any loss suffered by anyone as a result of action or omitting to act as a result of the material contained in the sample documents provided here and elsewhere in the book.

Dated ....**200[   ]**

[Details of Selling Shareholders to be inserted]

and

[Details of Purchasing Company to be inserted]

Draft Acquisition Agreement relating to the Sale and Purchase of the Entire Issued Share Capital of [Target Company to be inserted] Limited

Sandgate House
102 Quayside
Newcastle Upon Tyne
NE1 3DX

Contents

Clause

18. Further Assurance

Schedule I

Schedule 2

Schedule 3

Schedule 4

Schedule 5

Schedule 6

Schedule 7

Schedule 8

Schedule 9

This Agreement is made the   day of   200 [   ].

Between

(1) The seller ('the Seller') and

(2) The buyer ('the Purchaser')

1. **Interpretation** Sets out the definitions of terms to be used throughout the contract, which are then usually shown with an initial capital letter in the text (eg Completion in 5 below).

2. **Sale of Shares** Defines what is being sold, eg specifies the shares to be transferred.

3. **Consideration** How much is to be paid for the shares, typically a specified amount and then a reference to uplifts in respect of specific clauses (eg stock at value).

4. **Conditions Precedent** Any specific conditions required such as passing of a resolution to allow the sale, any reference to competition or regulatory authorities permissions etc.

5. **Conduct of Business Pending Completion** Sets out specific responsibilities in the period prior to Completion (eg that the seller will carry on trading as normal, keep the insurance up to date and not sell off major assets or make any other significant changes).

6. **Completion** Details of how and when Completion will take place and what the parties have to do to allow this to happen and the fallback options if there are any problems in delivering documents etc.

7. **Completion Balance Sheet** How (and when) the Completion accounts which determine the final purchase price (eg in respect of stock values) are going to be drawn up and what happens about any disputes.

8. **Warranties and Representations** The Warranties given by the Sellers to the Purchaser which will generally include that:

   ◆ the Sellers have the power and authority to sell the shares
   ◆ the Warranties given will be true, accurate and not misleading and will continue to be so at the time of Completion
   ◆ each Warranty is separate and independent of the others
   ◆ if you qualify any Warranty as being to the best of your knowledge, this is after having made reasonable enquiries
   ◆ you accept that the Purchaser is relying on your Warranties.

   This will also set out that the Purchaser's rights in respect of any Warranties given:

   ◆ will not be altered by any knowledge that they had (other than what is in the disclosure letter) or any failure to claim immediately in respect of any breaches
   ◆ that the Warranties and representations are limited to those specified in the agreement that the rights of the Purchaser to claim under the Warranties will be limited by the terms of Schedule 5 (unless there has been fraud or misrepresentation).

9. **Restrictive Covenants** Sets out the commitment of each of the Sellers not to without the Purchaser's prior written consent:

   ◆ engage in a specified type of business (directly or indirectly) for a specified period and/or within a specified area
   ◆ entice away employees (particularly key ones who may be specified)
   ◆ solicit customers, business (or sometimes suppliers)
   ◆ use a similar business name.

   Confirms that these restrictions are separately enforceable and are considered reasonable to protect the goodwill of the business being purchased.

10. **Retention and Joint Account** How the Retention account into which a proportion of the sales proceeds are going to be paid will be dealt with and

how claims against this account by the purchaser should be made.

11. **Payments** That all payments made under the contract should be made in full without any set offs.

12. **Provisions Relating to this Agreement** General provisions about how the agreement is to be read and interpreted (eg that it is governed by English law).

13. **Announcements and Circulars** That no announcements about the sale other than any required by law or regulations should be made without the other side's consent.

14. **Entire Agreement** That this Agreement and its related schedules constitute the whole agreement and supersede any other documents or agreements (which can only be changed by written agreement of both sides). Also used to ensure that each party acknowledges that it is relying solely on the documents referred to in the agreement and not on any other representations.

15. **Subsequent Sale** A non-embarrassment clause that if the buyer sells on the company at a profit within a specified period, the buyer has to pay a proportion of the proceeds across to the seller.

16. **Costs** That each party bears its own costs in respect of the agreement.

17. **Notices** Details of where and how notices can be served on the other party and when they will be deemed to have been received.

18. **Further Assurance** A confirmation that where necessary, the sellers will (at the buyer's expense) execute any further documents that may be needed to complete the sale.

Schedule 1

The Sellers' Holdings

A table setting out the sellers' shareholding(s).

Schedule 2

Company Details

A table setting out details of the Company (Company number, date of incorporation, authorised share capital, directors, registered office, auditors, accounting reference date, etc).

Schedule 3

The Properties

A table setting out details of the freehold and leasehold properties owned by the company.

Schedule 4

Warranties

The detailed specific warranties that are being agreed, covering in a typical agreement say:

1. **Memorandum and Articles** The copy of the Memorandum and Articles of Association of the Company attached to the Disclosure Letter are correct, that the register of members and other statutory books have been properly kept, are up to date and the Seller has had no notification that there are any mistakes that need to be corrected.

2. **Options** That there are no outstanding options or other rights to the company's shares.

3. **Returns** That as far as the Sellers are aware the Company has complied with the provisions of the Companies Acts and has filed all statutory returns and notified all charges at Companies House.

4. **Commissions** That there is no liability for a brokerage or other fee outstanding in relation to a sale of the shares.

5. **Possession of Documents** That the Seller has all the original copies of all relevant documents (eg title deeds).

6. **Investigations** There are (as far as the Sellers are aware) no current or pending government investigations into the company (and no grounds for such an investigation known).

7. **Accounts Warranty** As far as required by the agreement, the Accounts have been drawn up in accordance with normal accounting conventions, have been prepared on the same basis as accounts for the last three years, give a true and fair view and meet the requirements of the Companies Act.

8. **Stock Valuation and Accounting Policies** That the stock in the accounts has been valued consistently with prior periods, at the lower of cost or net realisable value in accordance with the relevant accounting standard (SSAP 9) with adequate provision for obsolete or slow moving stock.

9. **Depreciation of Fixed Assets** That the fixed assets in the accounts have been

depreciated consistently in the last three years' accounts in accordance with the relevant accounting standard (SSAP 12).

10. **Accounting Reference Date** The Accounting Reference Date of the Company is as stated in Schedule 2.

11. **Book Debts** None of the debtors shown in the accounts are overdue by more than 90 days old or have (or should have) been written off as irrecoverable or credit notes issued.

12. **Books of Account** Full disclosure of all matters has been made to the auditors in drawing up audited accounts and the books and records are accurately prepared and complete.

13. **Capital Commitments** There are no outstanding commitments to capital expenditure (or disposal of capital assets).

14. **Dividends and Distribution** There have been no dividends or other distributions paid since the last balance sheet date.

15. **Bank and Other Borrowings** The Company has kept within its overdraft facility over the past 12 months and total borrowings have not exceeded any limitations imposed by its Articles, a debenture or regulatory requirements.

    All loans and debts have been repaid as they fall due and the company has had no formal or informal demands or notice to repay from any lender.

    The company has not created any loan capital or entered into any off balance sheet finance arrangements or discounted its debts.

16. **Loans by and Debts Due to the Company** The Company has not lent any money which has not yet been repaid to it, has not lent money other than in the normal course of business and has not made any loan or quasi-loan contrary to the Companies Acts (this is targeted particularly at Directors' loan accounts).

17. **Liabilities** So far as the Sellers are aware there are no liabilities outstanding (including disputed or contingent liabilities) other than those shown in the Accounts or incurred in the normal course of trading since the Balance Sheet Date.

    No one has claimed any security over assets and there are no disputes relating to any assets.

18. **Bank Accounts** Details of all the bank accounts and other accounts of a finance nature operated by the Company are set out in the Disclosure Letter.

19. **Continuation of Facilities** Full details of all the Company's financial facilities

(eg loans, overdrafts, letters of credit etc) are set out in the disclosure letter (with copies attached where relevant). The Seller is not aware of any default or demands for repayment.

20. **Effect of Sale of Shares** The Sellers have no reason to believe that as a result of the share sale:

   ◆ any supplier or customer will want to cease trading with the Company or wish to change its terms of trade,
   ◆ any key employees will wish to leave
   ◆ the Company will lose any specific rights
   ◆ the Company will breach any agreement or regulatory requirements
   ◆ anyone will be allowed to escape an obligation to the Company
   ◆ any debts or loans will be made to fall due for immediate payment or lead to any lender exercising their security (eg by appointing a receiver).

21. **Business since the Balance Sheet Date** The business has been carried on normally since the Balance Sheet Date with all transactions being recorded as normal, no major changes in the business's circumstances, customers, suppliers or turnover and the level of fixed assets maintained, no new borrowing taken on and all liabilities paid on normal due dates.

22. **Licences** So far as the Sellers are aware the Company has all its necessary licences and permits required to conduct its business, the Company complies with their requirements and the Seller is not aware of any breaches or other reasons why these might be revoked.

23. **Litigation** As far as the Sellers are aware neither the company nor any related party is engaged in any litigation and there is none pending against the Company or a related party (or any known grounds for proceedings).

   There are no disputes with the government, no outstanding or potential employee claims and as far as is known, no pending criminal prosecutions against any officer of the Company.

24. **Insolvency** The Company is not insolvent nor is it unable to pay its debts within the meaning of Section 123 of the Insolvency Act 1986. There are no outstanding judgements or court orders against the company; no one has taken any action to commence insolvency proceedings against the Company (liquidation, receivership or administration) and there are no proposals for a Company Voluntary Arrangement or other compromise with creditors.

25. **Insurances** Details of the insurance policies are set out in the Disclosure Letter, the premiums are up to date and the Seller is not aware of any outstanding claims.

26. **Fair Trading and Restrictive Practices** So far as the Sellers are aware the Company is not in contravention of any of the relevant competition legislation.

27. **Material Contracts** The Company has no contracts that are equivalent to more than 10% of its turnover or significant contracts that:

    ◆ the company is in breach of the contract terms
    ◆ might be cancelled as a result of the sale
    ◆ are loss making
    ◆ were entered into other than as part of part of normal business
    ◆ have significant currency or other risks or
    ◆ carry onerous terms or cannot easily be fulfilled.

28. **Grants** Full details of all grants and other such support are set out in the Disclosure Letter and the Seller is not aware of any grounds that would require repayment or forfeiture.

29. **Compliance with Contracts** The Company has complied with all contracts it has entered into and made all payments due.

30. **Defective Products** So far as the Sellers are aware the Company has not made or sold any defective products or had any notices under relevant consumer protection legislation.

31. **Service Liabilities** The Company has no outstanding liability (other than imposed by law) to service, repair, maintain or take back goods that are sold.

32. **Data Protection** The Company has registered under the Data Protection Act 1998 and complied with its requirements.

33. **Guarantees and Indemnities** There are no outstanding guarantees or indemnities given by the Company.

34. **Directors** The directors' details shown in Schedule 2 are correct.

35. **Pollution** So far as the Sellers are aware the Company has complied with relevant Environmental legislation, holds relevant licences and has no Environmental claims or liabilities.

36. **Employees and Terms of Employment** Full details of employees and their terms and conditions are set out in the Disclosure Letter. There are no other contracts (eg personal service contracts) and no binding agreements with trades unions or other bodies representing employees.

37. **Bonus and other Schemes** There are no bonus or profit share schemes or other discretionary payments made.

38. **Service Contracts** There are no contracts containing notice periods of over one month or including payments on termination in excess of the statutory minimums.

39. **Disputes with Employees** There are no outstanding or potential disputes with claims against the Company by employees or ex-employees as far as the Sellers are aware.

40. **Agreements with Unions** There are no agreements or other agreements (whether or not legally binding) between the Company and any trade union or other body representing employees.

41. **Change in Remuneration** There have been no significant changes in employees' terms of employment or their pay made or discussed since the Balance Sheet Date.

42. **Redundancies** No employee will become redundant and be entitled to a redundancy payment as a result of any provision of this Agreement.

43. **Pensions** Full details of all pension schemes are set out in the Disclosure Letter (and there are no other such schemes), together with:

   ◆ copies of the relevant deeds and schemes rules
   ◆ membership details
   ◆ benefit entitlements
   ◆ confirmation that:
      – contributions are up to date
      – insurance is in place to cover benefits
      – all advisory costs have been paid up to date
      – there are no other liabilities and no actual or pending claims or litigation in respect of the scheme.

44. **Assets and Charges** The Company owns all the assets to be sold and there are no outstanding liabilities or charges attached to any of the assets.

45. **Stock and Work in Progress** Levels of stock are adequate but not excessive, the stock is properly identified and is in good usable or saleable condition (except where already provided for as slow moving or obsolete).

46. **Leased Assets** There are no grounds under which leased assets are at risk of being repossessed.

47. **Plant and Machinery** The company owns and controls all the plant, machinery, vehicles and other equipment to be sold, subject to any leasing or HP agreements shown in the disclosure letter.

48. **Tax Provisions** The Company has made proper provision (taking account of the

relevant Accounting Standards) for all tax and deferred tax liabilities.

49. **Administration** All tax returns, computations and payments due have been made or paid by the due dates and are full and accurate. No material tax liabilities have arisen since the balance sheet date and the Company has properly operated its PAYE accounting system.

50. **Taxation Claims, Liabilities and Reliefs** Full details of any and all tax claims that may be made by the Company and all potential tax liabilities are set out in the disclosure letter.

51. **Distributions and Deductability of Payments** The Company has not redeemed any shares or paid any distributions or dividends since the Accounts Date.

It has not received or made any payments which may be disallowable for tax purposes or which would give rise to a capital gain.

52. **Close Companies** The Company has always been a close company as defined by tax legislation and has complied with the requirements for this type of company.

53. **Group Relief and Surrender of Surplus ACT** The Company has not been a member of a group or an associated company of another at any time in the last six years.

54. **Capital allowances** All expenditure on plant and machinery qualifies for writing down allowances and has not elected to treat any assets as short life assets.

55 **Transactions not at arm's length** The Company has not undertaken any transactions at undervalue or not at arm's length.

56. **Base values and acquisition costs** The values used for capital assets will be such that no chargeable gains arise as a result of the sale.

57. **Tax avoidance** The Company has not engaged in or been a party to any tax avoidance schemes.

58. **Unremittable income and capital gains** The Company has no income that falls within the category of 'unremittable income' under tax legislation.

59. **Demergers** The Company has not been involved in a demerger.

60. **Transfer of overseas trade** The Company has not transferred any part of its business overseas.

61. **Sale and leaseback of land** The Company has not entered into any sale and leaseback of land arrangements.

62. **Stock dividends and deep discount securities** The Company has not owned or issued any 'deep discount' securities.

63. **Controlled foreign companies** There are no grounds for the Inland Revenue to direct that profits are apportionable to a foreign company.

64. **Chargeable gains** The rules to be applied to determine the Company's potential corporation tax liabilities.

65. **Capital losses** The Company has not incurred a capital loss involving a connected person.

66. **Acquisition from group members** The Company does not own any assets purchased from a company with which it was in a group at the time.

67. **Replacement of business assets** The Company has not made claims under tax rules relating to roll over relief, replacement of business assets etc.

68. **Gifts involving group companies** The Company has not received any assets by way of gift.

69. **Gains accruing to non-resident companies** The Company has no gains that may be liable to tax as a non-resident company.

70. **Value Added Tax (VAT)** The Company has registered for VAT and:
    ◆ maintains accurate records
    ◆ has complied with the requirements of the tax
    ◆ is up to date with payments
    ◆ has no outstanding penalties or notices
    ◆ is not part of a group
    ◆ does not operate any partial exemption recovery method
    ◆ the disclosure letter gives full details of any bad debt relief being claimed.

71. **Inheritance Tax (IHT)** The Company has made no transfers of value and there are no outstanding IHT charges.

72. **Stamp Duty** All stamp duty liabilities have been paid and no claims for relief have been made in the last five years.

73. **Title** That the property details set out in Schedule 3 are correct, the Company has good title to any freehold land and is not occupying any properties not declared on Schedule 3.

74. **Restrictions and Encumbrances** The Company has full rights to occupy the properties and there are no onerous restrictions or covenants.

75. **Town and Country Planning and related matters** The Properties are currently used for the purposes set out in Schedule 3 and this use is authorised under relevant regulations covering planning, public health, building regulations etc.

76. **Adverse Orders** No notices have been received adversely affecting the current use of the Properties.

77. **Disputes and Access** The Sellers are not aware of any disputes regarding boundaries or access.

78. **Leasehold Property** The Company is up to date with its rent, there are no rent reviews outstanding and it has not contravened any material conditions of its leases

79. **Statutory Obligations** The Company has met all its obligations under all relevant law (such as fire precautions, public health, environmental protection, factories acts etc) and there are no outstanding notices.

    The rateable value of the Properties is set out in the disclosure letter.

80. **Intellectual Property Rights (IPR)** The Company is the sole owner of the IPR that it uses and where appropriate this has been registered in the company's name within the relevant countries and the registrations maintained.

    That the company has kept its IPR confidential, has not given any third party rights over the IPR, is not aware of any infringements (and has not infringed any other parties' IPR) and is not party to any secrecy agreements in respect of other parties' IPR.

81. **Shares** That the Company does not own (or is committed to buy) shares or bonds in any other company.

82. **General** That all the information provided by the Sellers' Solicitors to the Purchaser's Solicitors as written replies to their pre-contract enquiries was and still is true and accurate in all respects.

Schedule 5

Warranty Limitation Provisions

1. The Seller's maximum total liability is limited to the sale Consideration.

2. The Purchaser can only make a claim if the total liability exceeds a specified amount (but any such claim will be for the whole amount).

3. The Sellers have no liability where the amount is less than a specified sum.

4. The Sellers have no liability unless claims are made in writing (with full details) within the specified period.

5. The Sellers have no liability for matters arising out of actions taken after the date of completion or matters set out in the disclosure letter.

6. The Sellers have no liability if the purchaser fails to take their advice in dealing with any dispute or claim.

7. The Purchaser cannot make a claim arising solely from any changes in prevailing rates of taxation.

8. If the Sellers settle any claim that the Purchaser is subsequently able to recover from a third party the purchasers will reimburse the Sellers (net of costs).

9. The Purchaser will advise the Seller as soon as practical once the Purchaser becomes aware of any circumstances that may give rise to a claim under the Warranties and keep the seller notified of developments and provide copies of relevant information.

10. The Purchaser will take actions (at the Seller's cost) that the Seller reasonably requests to deal with any situation that may give rise to a Warranty claim.

11. The Purchaser cannot settle any matter giving rise to a Warranty claim without having complied with the above requirements.

12. The purchaser cannot claim unless it shall have first complied with the provisions of paragraph 9 and 10 of this Schedule.

13. Any claim will be reduced by the extent to which it is covered by insurance or has only arisen as a result of changes in law, taxation or accounting policies by the Company.

14. No Warranty Claims can be made except in respect of matters set out in this agreement.

15. The Sellers have no liability for anything specifically provided for in the completion balance sheet (to the extent of the provision made).

16. Payment of any Warranty Claim is in full and final settlement of that claim.

17. The Purchaser can only take action for damages in respect of any breach of the agreement and cannot rescind the sale.

18. Any overpayments of Warranties by the Sellers (eg in respect of tax) shall be repaid promptly once recovered by the Company.

19. Claims and payments made under the tax deed and warranties may be offset.

20. Neither the Purchaser or the Company will make any Warranty Claims against the Sellers except in accordance with this Agreement.

21. In assessing any damages or compensation payable by the Sellers the maximum value that can be put on the Company is the sale Consideration.

22. This agreement does not diminish the Purchaser's or the Company's duty to mitigate their loss.

Schedule 6

Completion Provisions

Part 1 – The Sellers' Delivers Obligations A list of what the Seller needs to deliver to the Purchaser (eg the executed tax deed, disclosure letter, share transfer forms, title documents etc).

Part 2 – The Sellers' Action Obligations A list of what the Seller needs to do (such as the passing of a board resolution to register the share transfers, arrange resignation of pension scheme trustees, arrange that specified directors enter into new service contracts etc).

Part 3 – Purchaser's Delivery Obligations A list of documents the Purchaser has to supply, usually limited to a counterpart Tax Deed, acknowledgement of receipt of the Disclosure Letter and a counterparty Power of Attorney.

Part 4 – Purchaser's Action Obligation A list of what the Purchaser needs to do including most importantly pay the consideration!

Schedule 7

Deed of Tax Covenant

Dated .... **200[ ]**

[Details of Selling Shareholders to be Inserted]

and

[Details of Purchasing Company to be inserted]

Deed of Tax Covenant

Sandgate House

102 Quayside

Newcastle Upon Tyne

NEW 3DX

This Deed is made the   day of   200[ ]

Between

(1) **the Sellers** and

(2) **the Purchaser**

Recital

This Tax Deed is entered into pursuant to the Agreement.

Operative Provisions

1. **Definitions** Definitions of the terms used.

2. **Covenant** That the Sellers undertake that they will pay the Purchaser the amount of the Company's outstanding tax liabilities as at completion.

3. **Exclusions** That the Sellers will not be liable to pay the Purchaser tax paid or provided for before completion or arising as a result of actions by the purchaser (such as failure to claim appropriate reliefs).

4. **Mitigation** If the Sellers have to pay the Purchasers under this agreement where there may be a right to reclaim such money, the Purchaser is obliged to pursue such a claim.

5. **Conduct of Claims** Details as to how the Purchaser notifies the Seller of a claim, the conduct of any claim by the purchaser and responsibility of the purchaser to deal on a timely basis to avoid unnecessary interest or penalties as well as to keep the seller advised.

6. **Dates for and quantum of payments** Period within which the Seller has to pay any claims.

7. **Deductions from Payments** Payments are to be made gross and without any set-offs.

8. **Savings** If it is found that the Company has made a saving on the taxation, the purchaser will pay over the saving to the Seller.

9. **Recovery from third Parties** If the Company is entitled to recover funds from third parties that reduce the Seller's liabilities then the Company will act to recover this (at the Seller's expense).

10. **Over-provisions** If the auditors certify that any tax has been over provided for in the Accounts then the purchaser will reimburse the Seller.

11. **Purchaser's Indemnity** The Purchaser gives the Seller an undertaking that it will ensure that the Company pays its taxation liabilities.

12. **General** That any payment by the Sellers under the Tax Deed will be treated

as a reduction in the sale Consideration and general terms about the Agreement (eg that it is governed by English law).

Schedule 8

Completion Balance Sheet and the Net Asset Statement

The Completion Balance Sheet and the Net Asset Statement prepared by the Seller's Accountants in accordance with normal accounting standards.

Schedule 9

Profit Earn-Out

Details as to how any profit earn-out is to be calculated (as it will normally be based on an adjusted net profit figure with specific exclusions), the amounts to be exceeded before any sum is payable and how and when it is to be calculated and paid.

Signature page

GOLDEN RULES SUMMARY

19. Expect to have to sign a non-competition covenant.

20. Expect to have to offer training or consultancy to the purchaser.

13

Keeping it from the Taxman

PLANNING PAYS

As you have traded your business over the years you will
undoubtedly have had to deal with a variety of taxes. Some of these
will relate to the ongoing trading of the business such as VAT or the
administration of PAYE in relation to employees' salaries. Whilst
there may be planning required in order to deal with these types of
taxes most efficiently and therefore minimise the tax burden on the
business, in essence these taxes arise out of the normal running of
the business and there is a limit to the strategic planning you can do
in respect of such taxes.

You may well find however that there are some areas of taxation
where it has paid to take advice and to develop a tax management
strategy so as to minimise the cost of such taxes to the business and
ultimately to yourself. For example many small businesses will take
advice around the area of Corporation Tax, Income Tax and
dividend policies so as to minimise tax payments. The owner-
manager often has a choice between paying themself a salary or a
dividend. The salary is subject to tax under PAYE, and to
employees' and employers' National Insurance contributions, but is
treated as a cost to the business before calculating the business's
Corporation Tax and it also sets the maximum level of pension
contributions that can be made into the director's pension scheme.
Alternatively, the director can forego salary. This reduces the
business's costs and will lead to the business paying Corporation
Tax on higher profits than would otherwise be the case, but will
allow the director to take income by way of a dividend, thereby

avoiding unnecessary National Insurance contributions.

Small businesses will often obtain the advice of their accountant in order to plan their approach to remuneration to obtain maximum tax advantages in respect of their current circumstances given the interaction of the Corporation and Income Tax systems.

When considering the sale of the business, rather than two taxes interacting there are essentially four. It is therefore doubly imperative that a business owner should seek professional advice over the tax planning of the sale.

This is a complex area and also one where any information given here will become out of date very quickly as the relevant rules, regulations, and rates of tax will vary from budget to budget, albeit that the basic principles tend to remain the same.

This chapter therefore sets out the four principal taxes to bear in mind when considering the tax planning of the business sale, and how their treatment differs between the sale of the shares in the business and the sale of the business's business and assets.

VALUE ADDED TAX

If your business is registered for VAT, when you sell items of stock, or services, or any business assets, such as plant and equipment or furniture, these are taxable supplies on which VAT (currently 17.5%) should be charged.

There is however an exception made to this where a business is being sold as a going concern to a VAT registered purchaser, in which case the business and assets can be sold without the need to charge VAT to the purchaser. Any such sale of assets will however have to clearly pass the tests that satisfy HM Customs and Excise that the sale is outside the scope of VAT. It is not uncommon, therefore, for example in sales of business and assets by receivers, to find a clause included stating that the sale is of a going concern and it is therefore to be outside the scope of VAT, but in the event that it is ruled to be within the scope of VAT, the purchaser will have to pay VAT on the consideration.

In the event of a sale of the shares of a company, VAT does not apply.

STAMP DUTY

Stamp Duty is a tax that applies to the sale of a wide range of assets at differing rates. In the event of the sale of shares in a company, Stamp Duty of 0.5% is payable at current rates, whilst on the sale of business and assets, Stamp Duty will be payable at varying rates on the varying class of assets included in the sale.

One way therefore to minimise Stamp Duty implications of the sale of business and assets is by excluding certain assets. If a sale of business and assets, for example, included the sale of the debtor book to the purchasers, Stamp Duty would be payable on the value of that book. Alternatively, the seller may exclude debtors from the deal, and may instead collect in the debts and thereby avoid Stamp Duty arising on the sale. In this circumstance, the purchase price would obviously be less (as the purchaser is not getting the benefit of the collection of debtors), but if the seller retains this asset they can collect the cash from the book as it comes in.

CAPITAL GAINS TAX

Capital Gains Tax is intended as a tax on the sale of assets which have been held over time (as opposed to Income or Corporation Tax which is charged on the profits of trading on a regular basis). Both companies and individuals may be liable for Capital Gains Tax.

The trend over recent years has been to reduce the impact of Capital Gains Tax on business sales. Where an individual has held shares for over two years, the Capital Gains Tax payable in respect of the value of those shares is reduced by a mechanism known as tapering relief down to an effective tax relief, at the time of writing of approximately 10%, on the sale of those shares.

If however the company sells its assets, any capital gain arising on the value of those assets will be chargeable to Capital Gains Tax at the company's rate of Corporation Tax (for example, 21%).

INCOME TAX

Where individuals have sold their shares in the company, there is no Income Tax implication as the entire taxation has in effect been dealt with through any capital gain that has arisen.

Where, however, the company has sold its business and assets, there then remains the problem of distributing this money out to the shareholders. If the company distributes this out by way of say a dividend, then this distribution will obviously represent taxable income in the hands of the shareholders and may therefore be taxed at their personal tax rate (for example for a higher rate taxpayer, at 40%).

It is clearly therefore much more tax efficient for the business owner to sell their shares in the business as if they have held these for over two years, they will only pay 10% Capital Gains Tax as opposed to the company selling its business and assets (and paying Capital Gains Tax on any profit on disposal at say 21%), before then having to distribute the proceeds by way of a dividend on which the owner will then pay Income Tax (for example, at 40%).

There are mechanisms which can be used in order to minimise or eliminate the Income Tax due in respect of distribution of proceeds from the company to the owners. For example, a member's voluntary liquidation (that is a solvent liquidation of the company) in which the assets of the dissolved company are simply distributed to the shareholders in settlement of their shareholding, can be used to reduce their tax rate.

However, since a sale of shares is so much more tax efficient than a sale of business and assets, this is the route which most business owners would seek to use to sell the business. As previously demonstrated, most business purchasers will seek a purchase of business and assets so as to minimise the risk of acquiring unknown or contingent liabilities. Given the potential difference in tax treatment, if a purchaser wishes to purchase a business and assets rather than the company, then this will be reflected in the price at which the owner is prepared to sell.

Of course, if there is any ongoing consultancy work or other payments following the sale, the seller is likely to be subject to Income Tax in respect of these.

The basic points are summarised in the table below, however the overriding rule must be to take professional advice at the outset as to how the deal can be best structured to meet your personal tax planning requirements.

	Sale of shares	Sale of assets
Value Added Tax	n/a	17.5% on taxable supplies (if registered) unless transaction is a sale as a going concern
Stamp Duty	0.5%	Range of charges dependent on asset sold
Capital Gains Tax	If held for more than two years, tapering relief applies, reducing tax rate to 10%	Company chargeable to tax at its effective rate of Corporation Tax on profit on disposal (eg at 21%)
Income Tax	n/a	Distribution of proceeds to shareholders (eg by way of a dividend) of taxable income for the shareholders at their effective rate of tax (eg 40%) An ongoing consultancy payment to the seller post sale will be subject to Income Tax in the normal way

Figure 21. Summary of business sale transaction.

Log onto www.creativefinance.co.uk for referral to an appropriate tax advisor or to an insolvency practitioner in respect of a member's voluntary liquidation, if needed.

GOLDEN RULE 21

Take tax advice

There is not much point in negotiating 5% up or down on the price you are selling for if you have not planned the sale so as to pay 10% tax rather than 40%.

GOLDEN RULES SUMMARY

21. Take tax advice.

And Then What?

Well congratulations, you have sold your business and I hope achieved your objectives. So the next question is: then what?

Hopefully at an early stage in this process you will have decided on your objectives in selling the business, whether these be retirement or freeing you up to pursue some new venture. As part of this process, before selling your business it is useful to go and talk to other people who have been through this process to find out how they have coped with the change of circumstances. Even if you remain in your business you must appreciate that circumstances are going to change significantly. People who pretend to themselves (or worse still, tell their staff) that everything will go on exactly as before are often the most disappointed in the aftermath of the sale.

Obviously everyone's circumstances are different, but having concluded a sale you need to be thinking about the following.

HOW DO YOU SECURE YOUR FUTURE OUT OF THE PROCEEDS OF THE SALE?

Where the sale has resulted in the capturing of a significant element of wealth that had previously been tied up in your business being converted into cash or shares in the acquiring company, you need to consider how you diversify this portfolio into a range of assets to provide you with income and capital going forwards. You may already have a pension scheme set up which you wish to ensure is funded; you may wish to develop your investments in other stocks and shares or in property. The important point is that just as you have taken advice in order to achieve the maximum value from selling your business, you should at the same time be taking advice as to how you obtain the maximum value from the money you get for it. I therefore recommend that you speak to an independent financial advisor as to the appropriate investment strategy for you given your circumstances and your objectives going forwards.

See www.creativefinance.co.uk for referral to an Independent Financial Advisor for access to financial services.

DO YOU HAVE A FUTURE INTEREST IN BUSINESS?

If you have sold your business in order to concentrate on new or other business interests, then you already have an ongoing interest in other businesses. However many people sell up in order to 'retire' but wish to remain involved in business or find, after a period, that they miss the involvement and stimulation that being in business gives them.

If the sale has given you sufficient cash resources that you have secured your future and have significant surplus funds available to invest, you might want to consider becoming what is known as a **business angel**, as a way of investing your money, retaining an interest in business, and in some cases acting to 'give back' into the community some element of support and backing that you may have received in the past (or wished you had done). A business angel invests typically in small or start-up businesses that require some capital to get off the ground but are too small to attract venture capitalists and are unable to attract bank funding due to their lack of assets. Business angels differ in their approach in that they will generally seek to be involved hands on with the company and have an active, if non-executive role at director level and in marketing the business to their contacts. Typically business angels look to operate within an industry that they know and have experience and a wide range of contacts in.

Alternatively a number of business agencies, such as local Business Links, run mentoring services where they seek the advice and support of experienced business people to give guidance to younger people or new businesses starting up on a no or low cost basis.

However if you are investing or seriously involved in running a new business, appreciate that this will always have some risk attached.

Warning case study

Mr X sold his business and made a significant capital gain. He decided that he would continue to be involved in business by acting as a business angel and invested in a small business, taking on the role of finance director.

After four months the business collapsed as a result of fraud by the managing director. The liquidator investigated the company's affairs and decided that there was sufficient evidence to pursue all the directors for wrongful trading, including Mr X.

In practice, Mr X was the only director with sufficient personal wealth to be worth suing and so the only director who ended up having to settle a substantial claim in the liquidation was Mr X, not the fraudulent managing director.

ARE YOU THINKING OF BUYING A BUSINESS?

Having used this book to help you to sell, hopefully it will also be of assistance to you in considering any business purchase you may wish to make.

HOW WILL YOU COPE WITH RETIREMENT?

You may fantasise about how relaxed life is going to be once you have given up the cares of running your own business and you may well be looking forward to being out on that golf course or that long and well deserved holiday in the south of France. And why not take a break? You deserve it.

But it is well to be prepared for the fact that having run and built businesses over many years, many people find the shock of the change of circumstances following the sale, and the lifting of the day-to-day imperatives of running the business, quite difficult to cope with. Going from working very full time to having a lot of free time on your hands, being at home with your family for much longer periods than previously, feeling perhaps that you are at a loose end and not being relied on by hundreds of people for decisions all the time, can be quite disorientating. You really must try to ensure that you are as mentally prepared as possible for that change in circumstances.

Again, talk to people who have gone through the process of selling their businesses and find out how they coped with the change. This is another reason why staying on with your business in some form of winding down consultancy for a period of time, so that you can 'ease yourself' into retirement, can be a sensible idea.

Alternatively you may wish to consider actively taking up new areas of interests and activities, be they social, practical, religious, sporting, or business, prior to getting into the process of selling your business, so that as you let go of your business, you have other things to engage your time.

The 21 Golden Rules

A SUMMARY

My golden rules for achieving a successful sale as set out in the preceding chapters are as follows.

Golden rule 1: Have a good reason to sell (that is logical to the buyer)

The buyer will want to know why you are selling. The more valid your reason for selling, the more serious the buyer will be. If you do not appear to have a valid reason for selling, the buyer will be suspicious and think you are selling because there is something wrong with the business that they have not yet spotted or you are not serious about selling. If they are suspicious about the business they will not pay you as much for it.

Golden rule 2: Be serious about selling

Don't be for sale until you are for sale. Ensure that buyers know that they have a one-off opportunity to deal with a serious seller who is committed to go through with the process of selling and won't waste their time and money.

Golden rule 3: Choose your moment to sell, do not have it forced upon you

Be proactive about deciding when you want to sell your business. Never allow yourself to become a forced seller of your business as a result of economic or other reasons as you will achieve a worse price because first, you will not be selling at the most opportune moment to maximise value, and second, anxiety will force you to accept worse offers than you would otherwise consider.

Golden rule 4: Start early

You are only going to sell this business once, so it does pay to do it right first time. This sale is like any other sales process, you have to know your product, prepare it so it is attractive for prospective customers, get to know the needs and wants of your prospective purchasers, and sell them the product, pursuing it all the way through to doing the deal.

Golden rule 5: Remember a valuation is just a valuation, your business is really worth (only) what someone is prepared to pay for it

At best a valuation is an opinion (ie, a best guess) as to what someone will pay for your business. The only true valuation with any real meaning is the deal that is actually eventually done when someone puts their hand in their pocket to pay. This may sometimes reflect issues that are completely outside a normal valuation basis.

Golden rule 6: Decide on your drop-dead price in advance

In addition to your target price for the business, you also need in mind a drop-dead price which is the amount below which you will not sell. Obviously this is a figure which you never, repeat *never*, disclose to the prospective purchaser.

Golden rule 7: Set a reasonable target price

Whatever valuation method you use, you should set a reasonable target price for your business. Setting a ridiculously high price can be a major mistake as:

♦ it may well scare away many potential buyers

♦ it tells people you are not very serious about selling your business

♦ it means your business may remain for sale for quite some time, which may lead potential buyers to think there is something wrong with your business which is preventing it from being sold; and

◆ it may well sour your post-deal relationship with the purchaser, which is a particular concern if you are expecting to have some involvement with the business after the sale.

Golden rule 8: First one to mention price, loses
As with all negotiations, it is usually best to wait for the other party to mention price first so as to avoid under or overpricing and to get some indication of their possible range of values.

Golden rule 9: Start early when grooming for sale
Allow yourself plenty of time to manage the business's profits so as to be able to clearly demonstrate proof of strong and growing profits.

Golden rule 10: Tidy up the physical plant
Don't forget that first impressions count. If you put yourself in the buyer's shoes and were to visit your premises today for the first time with the thought 'Should I buy this business?' how impressed would you be? Does your plant look tidy, with everything in its place and work flowing through well maintained machines efficiently and in a controlled manner? Or is it chaotic, stock looking untidy, machines looking in need of a lick of paint or maintenance?

Golden rule 11: Once you've got it looking good, keep it looking good
As you go through the sales process remember that until you have actually sold the business it is not sold. So don't let either your operations or the way you are presenting your plant and equipment slip as you go through the process. Keep the business looking attractive, keep the hours being worked normal, keep the stock at the

appropriate levels, right up until the time when you have signed on the dotted line and collected the cash.

Golden rule 12: Avoid surprises

There is nothing that causes more problems in the sales process than an unexpected surprise discovered late in the day. Thorough prior preparation of your business, its leases, contracts, documents, title deeds and so on, helps prevent unnecessary surprises.

Golden rule 13: Get the best help available

Good professional advisors cost money. But good professional advice makes you more money than it costs. Selling your business is probably the most important single transaction you will ever undertake, do you really want to do it on the cheap? For a recommendation, email markb@reinventyourbusiness.co.uk.

Golden rule 14: Be an active part of the sales process

Whilst your advisors may handle much of the practicalities of contacting prospective purchasers and getting them interested, they will be relying on you to make time to meet with prospective purchasers who are interested in buying your business, and the advisor's own staff who need to talk to the horse's mouth about all aspects of the business, and follow your advisor's advice about dealings with prospective purchasers.

Golden rule 15: Understand that buyers want certainty

Much like buying a secondhand car, the thing that your buyer fears the most is that they are buying a 'pup' that you are getting rid of before some inevitable collapse or crisis comes home to roost. Your job is to be sympathetic to these concerns and do everything in your power to make them comfortable that they know sufficient about the long-term prospects and risks of the business to be able to invest in it.

Golden rule 16: Be flexible, patient and proactive in negotiation

Putting together the perfect deal is difficult and achieving a successful sale will require both parties to be flexible and creative in negotiation. Once an offer has been received, study it carefully and come back with your constructive counter-offers to help create a win-win situation for both sides and to keep the ball rolling.

Golden rule 17: Be prepared to finance

Insisting on an all-cash deal is likely to reduce the number of potential buyers and suggests that you may lack confidence in the future of the business. Financing the sale may mean you achieve a higher price, may help you in the timing of cash receipts for tax purposes, and allow you to earn interest as a separate element of income, but ensure you obtain enough initial cash.

Golden rule 18: Terms are as important as price

Since the negotiation of price is not simply about price, but also about broad terms of the deal, in addition to your target and drop-dead price, you must have given thought to the objectives you are trying to achieve and your views as to your preferred deal terms including the warranties you are prepared to give before getting into these negotiations.

Golden rule 19: Expect to have to sign a non-competition covenant

Since you have built this business up and know all the suppliers and customers, what is the value of your business to the purchaser if you go out the day after the sale and simply set up a new business, contacting all those suppliers and customers again? In order to protect the value of their investment, every purchaser will be looking for some form of non-competition agreement.

Golden rule 20: Expect to have to offer training or consultancy to the purchaser

Having built the business up, much of the knowledge about how it works, its know-how, and its customer relations will inevitably reside in your head. In order to obtain value from the business, the purchaser is going to need to have you transfer that knowledge, skills, know-how, introductions, contacts, and so on across to them as the new owner of the business. This may require you to stay on to give a short period of training over a few weeks in how the business operates, or to stay on for a longer period of say two years, to act as a consultant introducing the new owners to the customers and gradually handing over these relationships.

Golden rule 21: Take tax advice

There is not much point in negotiating 5% up or down on the price you are selling for if you have not planned the sale so as to pay 10% tax rather than 40%.

THE THREE WORD SUMMARY

Overall, a successful business sale is really a matter of three Ps:

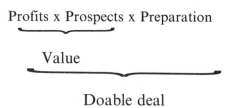

$$\frac{\text{Profits x Prospects x Preparation}}{\text{Value}}$$

Doable deal

- ◆ **Profits** – demonstrating what the business really makes as a profit for its owner.

- ◆ **Prospects** – demonstrating how healthy and well positioned for the future the business is so that it will go on making profits.

Together these deliver value.

◆ **Preparation** – being well prepared to deal with the sale process.

Adding preparation to value leads to a doable deal.

CONTACTING THE AUTHOR

I hope that this book has been of use to you in preparing to engage in selling your business and helps you to achieve the best value from your sale.

I am always interested in feedback and suggestions for consideration in future editions, or to provide help and assistance, so please feel free to contact me on 01388 528913 or markb@reinventyourbusiness.co.uk.

Glossary

HOW TO WHITEWASH YOUR BIMBO – A GLOSSARY OF CORPORATE FINANCE TERMS

Like any other area of activity, the buying and selling of businesses has its own jargon. This section sets out brief explanations for some of the common terms used.

AIM The alternative investment market, a public UK stock market which has lower criteria for obtaining a listing than a full stock market listing.

asset based finance Lending that is based on specific classes of asset, eg commercial mortgages based on property, factoring or invoice discounting based on debtor book (and sometimes stock), leasing, hire purchase, or chattel mortgages based on plant and machinery. Often an important element in the financing of buy-outs. Advice and financing can be obtained through independent financial asset brokerages (try www.creativefinance.co.uk)

BIMBO See buy-out

Book value The value of assets as shown in the accounts of the company. As book values are generally based on the historic cost of the asset less depreciation since it

was purchased, they often bear little or no relation to the asset's current market value.

Business angel A wealthy individual, often a retired businessman who has already sold one business who is interested in investing funds personally in smaller or start-up companies. Will often be looking for an active role in management of the company.

Buy-in See buy-out.

Buy-out The sale of your business to continue as a standalone entity (ie not a sale to a trade purchaser). Buy-outs come in a number of flavours. A management buy-out (MBO) is where the existing management team purchase the business from the shareholders; a management buy-in (MBI) is where a team of external managers buy out the shareholders to take over the running of the business; and a buy-in/management buy-out

(BIMBO) is where a mixed team of existing internal managers and external managers buy the business. Many buy-outs are backed by venture capital firms and are therefore 'financial sales'.

Contingent liability A potential liability of the business which may arise as a result of some specific event happening.

Data room A facility made available to a purchaser and their advisors where company information can be inspected.

Disclosure letter A letter usually attached or referred to in the sales contract that specifies certain items of information, such as exceptions to any general warranties given.

Discounted cashflow The value of money to be received in future periods, discounted back to its equivalent today (as money to be received at some future date is by definition less certain and therefore less valuable than cash in the hand now).

Due diligence The purchaser's process of detailed investigation and review prior to completing a purchase.

EBIT Earnings before interest and tax. The underlying profit from trading, before it is affected by the business's tax status or financing.

('Earnings' is an American term and the UK equivalent is PBIT – profit before interest and tax.)

EBITDA Earnings before interest, tax, depreciation, and amortisations, used as a measure of the 'cash' generated by trading activities.

Equity gap The perceived difficulty of raising funds for businesses where there is insufficient security available to obtain bank lending, but where the share capital required is below the level at which venture capital firms will generally be interested.

ERRP Estimated restricted realisation price. The estimated value of property or an asset given the restricted time within which to sell it (generally six months for a property, three months for plant and equipment). Replaces the older term 'forced sale value'.

ERP Estimated realisation price. The estimated value of a property or cost given a reasonable time within which to achieve a sale.

Escrow Placing on trust. Usually used in respect of an 'escrow account' where part of the sales proceeds will be held by a third party (eg a solicitor) for a specified period, so that in the event that the purchaser has a claim against the seller, they know there are funds available against which to claim.

Exclusivity clause A contractual

clause usually seen in heads of agreement that gives the purchaser exclusive rights to negotiate a deal with the seller.

Forced sale value See ERRP.

GAAP Generally accepted accounting practice. This means that your accounts have been prepared in accordance with normal accounting conventions. Note that American and UK GAAP have some significant differences and you will need professional advice if this is an issue.

Gearing Borrowing. A company is said to be highly geared (in US: leveraged) if it is largely funded by way of loans rather than share capital.

Going concern value The value of a group of assets to a continuing business based on not only the cost of the assets but their economic value as a productive unit to make the owners' profits into the future.

Goodwill The difference between the fair market value of assets acquired and the purchase price.

Grooming The process of preparing a business for sale to make it attractive to a purchaser. Can take up to two years.

Heads of agreement The document that sets out the price that has been agreed for the sale and the key terms, subject to due diligence and contract.

Heads of terms See heads of agreement.

Information memorandum See sales pack

Insolvency Being unable to pay debts as they fall due. The Insolvency Act sets out a number of tests including failure to deal with a statutory demand or to pay a judgement debt, and liabilities exceeding assets, each of which would be taken by a court as proof of insolvency.

IPR Intellectual property rights.

IRR Internal rate of return, the discount rate at which a net present value calculation gives a zero result, which in turn means that the discount rate equates to the return generated by the project or investment.

IPO Initial Public Offering, the American term for a flotation; taking and listing a company for the first time on a stock exchange.

Letter of intent See heads of agreement/heads of terms

Listing Floating a company on a public stock exchange.

Net present value A discounted cashflow, less the amount of money you have to pay to acquire it.

Non-embarrassment clause The right to share in any increased sales proceeds if your buyer sells your business on again within a specified time.

OFEX A privately traded listing where shares are dealt in on the basis of individual trades. Often used by small companies to obtain speculative money as an alternative to venture capital, but is significantly less liquid than other stock market listing as there are no active market makers trading the shares.

Open market value How much an asset will fetch if sold in the open market. See also ERP. Also known as fair market value.

PBIT See EBIT.

P/E ratio The price to earnings ratio which is how many times the current level of earnings someone is prepared to pay to acquire an interest in a company. A high P/E multiple usually indicates an expectation of high growth (ie, E is expected to grow significantly reducing the P/E ratio down to a more normal level). Inverse of yield.

Payback period How long it will take to recover an investment at current level of earnings.

Phoenix A buy-out from a liquidator or receiver by the existing management.

Post acquisition integration The process of change planned by a buyer in order to absorb the purchased business into their existing organisation.

Preference Putting one creditor in a better position than others. In the event of insolvency a liquidator will review transactions leading up to the liquidation and if certain conditions are met will seek to set aside any preferential transactions.

Prospectus A package of information prepared for provision to potentially interested investors in a flotation.

Sales pack A package of information prepared for provision to potentially interested parties.

Sales mandate An instruction to a corporate finance advisor to act to sell your business.

SAV Stock at value: Stock to be purchased at the value on the day of sale. Valuation will normally be determined by GAAP.

Secondary buy-out The sale of an interest in a company by one VC to another. Generally unpopular with VCs as it is seen as a sign of 'failure' by the first investing VC.

Section 320 Provision in the Companies Act that prevents a director purchasing substantial assets (broadly anything worth more than £100,000 or 10% of the net assets of the company) without first obtaining the consent of the shareholders.

Stock 1. A company's equity or share capital, colloquially: shares. 2. A company's trading stock comprising raw materials, work in progress and finished goods stock.

Target A company to be acquired.

Trade purchaser An industrial buyer of companies (as opposed to a financial purchaser such as a VC).

Transaction at undervalue Selling an asset at less than its fair value. In the event of an insolvency, a liquidator will review significant transactions preceding the insolvency and can act to set aside transactions at undervalue.

TUPE Transfer of Undertakings Protection of Employment Regulations: the rules which govern the treatment of employees on the sale of a business and which broadly make a purchaser responsible for taking on all the employees of the business being acquired (whether by sale of shares or business and assets) on the existing terms and conditions of service. Also provides that if employees have been made redundant in anticipation of, or in an attempt to avoid the purchaser having to take this responsibility, the purchaser will in any event be liable.

VC Venture Capital or Venture Capitalist.

Venture capitalists (VC) A firm set up to hold investors' money and to invest it in high growth opportunities.

Generally look to achieve a return of 30% per annum and hold investments for three to five years before selling. Generally tend not to be interested in deals below, say, £0.5million investment. (See equity gap; business angel.)

Whitewash agreement Section 161 of the Companies Act is designed to prevent asset stripping, by prohibiting the pledging or use of the company's own assets for the purchase of the company's shares (eg the purchaser cannot promise to pay the seller out of the proceeds of selling the company's assets once they have control of it, or borrow the money for the purchase by offering the company's assets as security). In many private company sales however, the only way that purchasers are able to raise funds to buy the company is by borrowing against the assets to be bought. An exception is therefore allowed to the 161 rule involving the preparation of a report by the company's auditors, known as a whitewash agreement.

Yield The amount of return received (E for earnings) for the price (P) paid. Usually shown as a percentage.

Useful Reference Sites

The following websites may be of assistance:

www.creativefinance.co.uk Asset-based finance brokerage able to assist in raising asset-based finance for MBO/MBI teams and referrals to specialist advisors in respect of corporate finance, tax or liquidations (if required for tax purposes) as well as independent financial advisors able to advise on pensions and investments. Contact finance@creativefinance.co.uk

www.horwathcw.co.uk Horwath Corporate Finance is the specialist division of Horwath Clark Whitehill, a major national accountancy firm, dealing with acquisitions and disposals, management buy-outs and buy-ins, capital raising, refinance and due diligence. Contact Adam Wardle on (020) 7842 7154 or Adam.Wardle@horwath.co.uk

www.insightassociates.co.uk Specialists in assisting to improve financial management of businesses, useful in starting to groom a business for sale. Contact Garry Mumford on (01279) 647447 or gmumford@insightassociates.co.uk

www.regenesispartners.co.uk Contact George Moore on (020) 8566 3811 or ghm@regenesispartners.co.uk. George Moore is an established company doctor with extensive experience in business sales, and in particular, sales of businesses in difficulty.

www.turnaroundhelp.co.uk Specific advice and assistance on turning around a business in difficulties if required prior to a sale. Contact help@turnaroundhelp.co.uk

www.wardhadaway.com leading multi-disciplinary legal and corporate finance practice covering all areas of business sales. Contact Ian MacDonald or Paul Duncan on ian.macdonald@wardhadaway.com or paul.duncan@wardhadaway.com on 0191 204 4000.

Index